Praise for

ALL THE WORLD'S A STAGE

"This is a love story. The story of a man whose love for performance and the written word, supported by a talented troupe of actors, dedicated professionals, and a legion of enthusiastic volunteers, has fostered that love and shaped it into one of this country's great festivals."

Rick Cluff

HOST, *THE EARLY EDITION*, CBC RADIO, VANCOUVER

"I wish to say thank you to Bard on the Beach for the many ways it has enriched the lives of the citizens of Vancouver. When I see those tents go up, I know that positive and good things are about to happen."

Philip Owen

FORMER MAYOR OF VANCOUVER

"Every once in a while a topic and a writer align perfectly. Seagrave's book is a must for all who marvel at Bard on the Beach and muse about the magic behind its success. A great read!"

Rick Antonson

PAST PRESIDENT AND CEO, TOURISM VANCOUVER

"A wonderful, well-deserved love letter to Vancouver's internationally renowned Bard on the Beach, as well as a savvy textbook on how to start and develop a world-class theatre and engage an audience and community. A must-read for every ambitious arts producer."

Jim Volz

PHD, CALIFORNIA STATE UNIVERSITY, FULLERTON; EDITOR, (INTERNATIONAL) SHAKESPEARE THEATRE ASSOCIATION'S *QUARTO*

"A lovely book—direct, unpretentious, filled with fact, fun, and anecdote. It is not just for the friends and faithful followers of Bard, who are legion, but for anyone interested in an object lesson in imagining the improbable and making it magnificent."

Max Wyman

WRITER, CRITIC, EDUCATOR, ADMINISTRATOR, AND ACTOR

"Every summer my English grandchildren come to Vancouver, and the first thing on their list of adventures is to check out what's playing at Bard on the Beach. *All the World's a Stage* is the perfect gift, for them, for me, and for everyone else."

Vicki Gabereau

CANADIAN RADIO AND TV PERSONALITY AND AUTHOR

JAYNE SEAGRAVE

Foreword by **JIM BOVARD**

ALL THE WORLD'S A ST☺GE

The story of VANCOUVER'S BARD ON THE BEACH

VICTORIA • VANCOUVER • CALGARY

Heritage House Publishing Company Ltd.
heritagehouse.ca

CATALOGUING INFORMATION AVAILABLE
FROM LIBRARY AND ARCHIVES CANADA

978-1-77203-176-8 (pbk)
978-1-77203-177-5 (epub)
978-1-77203-178-2 (epdf)

Edited by Kari Magnuson
Proofread by Karla Decker
Cover and interior book design by Jacqui Thomas
Cover and frontispiece photos by Jacqui Thomas
Interior photos courtesy of Bard on the Beach Theatre
Society, unless otherwise indicated.

The interior of this book was produced on
FSC®-certified, acid-free paper, processed chlorine
free and printed with vegetable-based inks.

We acknowledge the financial support of the
Government of Canada through the Canada Book
Fund (CBF) and the Canada Council for the Arts,
and the Province of British Columbia through
the British Columbia Arts Council and the Book
Publishing Tax Credit.

21 20 19 18 17 1 2 3 4 5

Printed in Canada

For the Bard volunteers

ACT IV   ACT V

ACKNOWLEDGEMENTS

My first debt must be to all involved with Bard on the Beach who enthusiastically embraced this project and gave me so much more than anticipated. At every level and in every capacity, I received unbridled support, enthusiasm, and commitment. This book is a testament to those individuals who told their stories to me. In stark contrast to anything else I have published, I am more than a little apprehensive about not having lived up to their expectations. It is a very different process writing a book that draws so heavily on the memories and experiences of others and not my own. In this respect, it has been a fascinating education in the arts and a different writing genre. I am therefore extremely grateful to all those at Bard on the Beach who granted permission to tell their stories, answered never-ending, often naive queries, and guided my way.

As always, Rodger Touchie and the wonderful staff at Heritage House Publishing not only offered encouragement from the outset to "run with the idea" and move away from travel writing, but also oversaw the creation of a book I think we can all be proud of. I continue to enjoy working with this eccentric publishing house, despite the endless teasing received from their CEO, whom I have known for over twenty years and now regard as a good friend and mentor.

My two teenage sons, Jack Seaberry and Sam Seaberry, and their father, Andrew Dewberry, supplemented this teasing while at the same time offering space and time for me to pursue the completely uneconomic and often lonely pursuit of writing over fifty thousand words in an eight-month period. They correctly rationalize that if I am engaged in the task of writing, I am unable to nag/pester/talk to them—a win-win situation. My family continues to provide stability and grounding to my eclectic, ever-changing literary and personal ambitions.

On July 1, Canada Day, 1992, I attended *Twelfth Night*, which was my first Bard on the Beach performance. Since that time, I have attended every year and seen most productions. My final "thank you" must therefore be to Christopher Gaze for not only offering so much support for this book but, more importantly, for having the vision and nerve to create a totally unique, magical Shakespeare festival for me and the population of Vancouver to enjoy every summer.

Jayne Seagrave
JANUARY 2017

FOREWORD

Bard on the Beach Shakespeare Festival means many things to many people. First and foremost, it is about art, theatre, and William Shakespeare. For the actors, it is about showcasing their talent and love of live theatre. For Bard's staff, it is about being part of a team and collaborating to support great art. For the volunteers, it means friendship, camaraderie, and proudly belonging to the Bard family. For the patrons, it is about seeing Shakespeare for the first time—or in a new way that makes them appreciate his genius even more. For youth, Bard offers an opportunity to grow skills and confidence through studying and performing Shakespeare.

And at its heart, Bard is living proof of the vision and determination of Christopher Gaze, who has led the Company since its inception in 1990. Under Christopher's watch, Bard has always been about collaboration and empowerment. At the same time, he has encouraged everyone to strive for excellence and contribute to creating extraordinary theatre in their own way.

These are the things that inspired me to become part of the Bard family, first as a patron and then as a Board member in 2008, taking on the role of Board Chair in 2012. I have been privileged to meet so many amazing people in the Company, many of whom have been interviewed for this book. So as I introduce it, I'm proud to salute all the people who have played their part in bringing Bard to life over the past twenty-eight years.

Many people have proposed over the years that the Bard story be documented, particularly before some of the leading players were no longer around to remember it accurately. But the circumstances needed to be right, and that is where Jayne Seagrave has timed her Bard entrance so perfectly.

This narrative is deeply influenced by Jayne's love of Bard. She has written with care, respect, and appreciation for what the Company has created, and what it has meant to her personally. For many years, she has been a keen observer of how the Festival has grown, and she has taken real pleasure in its versatility as it blossomed and flourished.

Jayne interviewed dozens of people in order to capture the stories and the culture of Bard and document the Festival's profound impact on Vancouver and beyond.

Now I invite you to enjoy the story she's crafted about the first twenty-eight years of our remarkable Festival—and may Bard's story continue to unfold and flourish!

Jim Bovard
CHAIR, BARD ON THE BEACH THEATRE SOCIETY

"*No legacy is so rich as honesty.*"

ALL'S WELL THAT ENDS WELL

PROLOGUE

‹ *Todd Thomson and Robert Olguin in* Twelfth Night, *2013.*

I should not be writing this book. While the idea to document the history of Bard on the Beach was essentially mine, it was my original intention to pass the writing on to another, more "artistic" individual with a creative, sensitive, performance-oriented passion. You see, I tended to think that if the definitive work—describing the history and growth of Canada's ninth-largest not-for-profit theatre company (the second-largest in British Columbia)—was to be written, it needed to be completed by someone in the arts. This individual would have, at the very least, in-depth knowledge of Shakespeare, and perhaps a career in and documented passion for the world's most popular playwright. Although I do like seeing live performances and have always made a point of attending Bard on the Beach on an annual basis, it would be a long stretch to describe myself as a "theatre buff." I see myself as far more practical, not that sensitive, having little in the way of artistic, creative, or theatrical talent. Indeed, my one and only "hands-on" theatrical experience was an acting role as Harry the Horse in a summer camp production of the musical *Guys and Dolls* over thirty years ago.

I cannot quote reams of Shakespeare or readily identify his characters, and I frequently get confused over the storylines and plots of each play. I admit that many times while watching Shakespeare, I drift off and think about the alcohol I want at intermission, what I am going to wear tomorrow, whether the man in front of me knows his breathing is really heavy, where the actress obtained those fantastic ankle boots, and whether I need to get gas on the way home. I like Shakespeare, but admit to finding some of his works heavy and confusing. I am not at all a Shakespeare aficionado. But I do genuinely really, really like theatre and adore the summer arrival of Bard on the Beach. In this respect, I feel I am not that different from many Vancouverites.

My enthusiasm, love, and intense admiration for Bard on the Beach and interest in its overriding success is two-fold: first, because I am its contemporary, and second, because I am fascinated with the way it has been successfully marketed and curious about how it has managed to achieve the cult status it enjoys today, which seems to elude so many other the-atre companies.

Bard's life in Vancouver perfectly mir-rors my twenty-seven years here and my evolution from poor immigrant to suc-cessful, established Vancouverite. Bard feels to me like a long-lost twin, or sensi-tive lover who understands my every feeling and can predict my thoughts and emotions, or best girlfriend who knows what I am about to say even before I open my mouth. As this theatre company was conceived and introduced, as it faltered, struggled, survived, grew, and became established in Vancouver, so did I. (Bard is actually one year older, having staged its first work—*A Midsummer Night's Dream*—

in 1990, whereas I arrived in the city a year later.) I have attended almost all produc-tions since 1991 and each year delight in seeing how the Company has changed and grown over the winter period, with either dramatic large-scale changes (a new tent, increased repertoire, pre-assigned seat-ing), or with smaller, barely discernible developments (better porta-potties with hand sanitizer, Bard chocolate, Starbucks coffee, the sale of Shakespeare-inspired jewellery).

So much of Bard's life parallels mine. For example, my first home in Vancouver was a small, one-bedroom, rented apart-ment; Bard's was a small, loaned tent. After a few years, I moved from my apartment to a 1917 fixer-upper house in Vancouver's east side and then, as fortunes changed, to a family abode on Vancouver's west side. Similarly, Bard's tent has grown in size and then in number—from one to two. As my home furnishings have gone from self-assembled to bespoke, so Bard's seating has progressed from hard, wooden benches to chairs loaned by the Vancouver School Board to padded, sponsored, pre-assigned comfort. As my diet has moved from fast food to west-end restaurants, so the food on offer at Bard has evolved from cans of pop to wine, from KitKats and licorice to

TOP ‣ *Bard Company, 1993.*

BOTTOM ‣ *Bard site gateway, 2015.*

logoed chocolate, and from sachet coffee to Starbucks. Like me, Bard's Artistic Director and founder, Christopher Gaze, arrived in Canada from England at the age of twenty-three. As his family, friends, and support network have grown, so have mine. And philosophically, we are similar. I share Bard's deep love and respect for the city of Vancouver, in which we chose to make our homes, have our children, and build our careers. The Canadian culture welcomed us and let us experiment, grow, and succeed. It allowed us opportunities to recognize and fulfill our dreams. I believe Bard and I share both an infatuation with Vancouver's beauty and a commitment to stay, give back, sing its praises, forgive its problems, and show it off to anyone who will pay attention.

My other fascination with Bard has been with its unique approach to marketing and the way it has managed to sell itself to the population of Vancouver and visitors. Unlike other theatre companies who depend significantly upon government support and Canada Council for the Arts grants to operate and survive, Bard's primary source of income is through ticket sales, corporate and individual donors, and selling to capacity crowds—a rarity in the theatre world in Vancouver and across the globe. Vancouverites believe in and love Bard. They were carefully, slowly courted to appreciate and support the Company. In 2013, TripAdvisor listed Bard as the fourth-best tourist attraction in Vancouver, while the Lonely Planet guidebooks included Bard in a list of the top ten Shakespeare festivals in the world. And all of this has been achieved in the space of relatively few years.

So it was because of my deep affinity for Bard that in 2015, while attending the London Book Fair in England and having lunch with Heritage House publisher Rodger Touchie, I suggested he commission a work on the story of Bard on the Beach. It was my intention to just supply the idea and for Rodger to find an "artsy" sort of writer from his vast bank of contacts to pen the work, but instead he suggested I move away from travel writing and consider it. Rodger rationalized I already had considerable experience writing about tents in many camping guides and it was only a slight departure to write about a much bigger tent. At that stage, I was not convinced. (Interestingly, as I spoke to more and more individuals associated with Bard during my research, references to camping were frequent, as many saw the experience of performing theatre in the elements as akin to camping.)

In July 2015, I met with Bard's Artistic Director, Christopher Gaze, and Executive Director, Claire Sakaki, to present the idea and inform them of Heritage House's interest in the project. I was also keen to determine if they were aware of anyone in the Bard community who would be interested in conducting the research and writing the text, someone who had expertise and knowledge of the theatre. I felt sure these two individuals so immersed in theatre would lead me to an appropriate writer.

They immediately supported the idea, commented on my enthusiasm, and surmised I should be the one to champion it, believing I could look at the organization with new eyes. At that moment, I got swept up in the joie de vivre, energy, and unconventionality that is characteristically Bard and, suddenly, working within the artsy community became appealing.

I have since been told that what I experienced is typical of Christopher Gaze. During my research, I was made aware of Christopher's ability to encourage participation in the Bard community through his energy and empowerment of the individual. As one Board member insightfully said, "So Christopher did to you what Christopher does to everyone." Another Board member explained Christopher's ability for enabling people and not holding on to things:

> *Christopher is wonderful at empowering and delegating—it's one of his great skills. He is not frightened at all at giving major decisions and responsibilities to people he believes he can trust. This empowers them. So you think, "Gee, if you have this confidence in me that you think I could do this, then I'm going to do a good job and I'm going to give that extra little bit," and that's what he gets out of people over and over again. And it happens at every level. It happens with the*

work you're doing, it happens with the Board, with staff. He knows their names; they are important. That personality he has is genuinely there with everyone. They matter to him.

This distinctive "Christopher trait" was identified not only by Board members but also by those in the artistic community, as a Bard designer shared with me: "When he speaks to you and gets you to do something, it's a combination of steamrolling and building you up." I had no hope. I had obviously fallen under his spell. (Had he applied some magic potion to my eyes, like a character from *A Midsummer Night's Dream?*) I enthusiastically committed to writing the story of an arts organization while possessing no proven track record in this writing genre.

Of course, like all projects undertaken with complete naiveté, it is not until the praise and encouragement has stopped and the writer is tasked with undertaking preliminary research that the true scale of the undertaking becomes apparent. Publishing contracts arrived with the request to deliver 48,000 words within an eight-month period. A preliminary fact-finding visit to the Vancouver Public Library revealed shelves upon shelves of Shakespeare texts. Who knew that in addition to studies on all thirty-nine actual plays and 154 sonnets, there was such a plethora of other works? Titles as diverse as *Shakespeare on Toast*; *Shakespeare for Young People*; *The Everyday Shakespeare*

Book; *Shakespeare's Sexual Language*; *A Feminist Companion to Shakespeare*; *Shakespeare Minus Theory*; *Shakespeare, Persia and the East*; *Shakespeare's Guide to Italy*; *Shakespeare and Youth Culture*; and, my favourite, *Shakespeare Is Hard, But So Is Life* (by Fintan O'Toole, who, within the first few pages of his tirade, informs the reader that over one thousand books on Shakespeare are published *every year*) crammed the stacks of the Vancouver Public Library. And every well-known writer seemed to want to get in on the act. Germaine Greer, the famous feminist, and Bill Bryson, the travel writer, to name but two, have both penned works on "the bard." Given that my eclectic, non-fiction *oeuvre* to date has involved an academic text on the police, a how-to guide on innovation and becoming a successful entrepreneur, numerous books on campgrounds in BC, and a solo woman's travel guide, it soon became apparent that my own contribution should not, in any capacity, attempt analysis of William himself. There were more than enough

TOP LEFT ‹ *Colleen Wheeler in* Elizabeth Rex, *2013.*

TOP RIGHT ‹ *Festival site gateway, 2015.*

BOTTOM LEFT ‹ *Box office staff, 2015.*

BOTTOM RIGHT ‹ *Moya O'Connell and Bob Frazer in* Hamlet, *2005.*

animals feeding at that literary trough. It was clear I needed to concentrate on the theatre group itself and the questions that intrigued me, in the hope that other Bard on the Beach enthusiasts would have the same interests.

I see Bard on the Beach as flawless. Each year, I attend the plays and it all seems to work like a well-oiled machine: a few hiccups, but, overall, amazingly successful. Bard marks the beginning of my summer—when I cycle by Vanier Park and see the distinctive tents under construction, I know that four nights will be spent within this wonderful, magical environment. But, at the same time, I have 101 questions. How and why did it start? How did it expand? To what do those involved attribute its success? What have been the failures, challenges, high points, low points? How and when are the plays chosen? How are the actors selected? Does everyone get on? Has there ever been a flop? Has there ever been a disaster? Does the City of Vancouver really appreciate what Bard has done for the tourism industry? Who makes the chocolates? Where do they get the costumes and those awesome shoes and boots? Who orders the merchandise for the gift shop? Who decides on the number of porta-potties needed, and on what data is this difficult decision made? Who decides where exactly to place the tents, how many volunteers are needed, and how they are recruited? When do auditions start? And, most importantly, what is done with all the unsold chocolate and un-drunk wine at the end of the season?

The aim of this book is to answer and address these and other questions. By interviewing a cross-section of the Bard community who have worked for the organization (either currently or in the past), I hoped to be able to provide these answers in an insightful, informative, and entertaining text in the true fashion of the distinctive Bard culture.

I am a trained social scientist and, following completion of a PhD in Criminology, taught research methods to undergraduate students at Simon Fraser University in Vancouver and to police officers in Manchester, England. This instruction involved teaching questionnaire design, interviewing techniques, and data analysis. In stark contrast to the rigid data-collection techniques I advocated to students, I am happy to report the information found in this book was not gathered in a strict, formal, structured, scientific way. After gaining full support and co-operation from Artistic Director Christopher Gaze and Executive Director Claire Sakaki for this work, I embarked on the interview process. Claire suggested current and former Bard staff and Board members (to which I added actors, directors, and designers) who had various lengths of experience on the Bard stage, and approached them on my behalf to ascertain if they were able to speak to me (some were working in other cities). I also spoke to volunteers and patrons during

Bard performances in September 2015, as well as volunteers identified by the Bard Volunteer Coordinator as having a number of years of experience. Interviews took place between October 2015 and May 2016.

My interview list snowballed as interviewees often recommended I speak to one of their colleagues. Interviews typically lasted between forty-five minutes and two hours and took place in the Bard offices, in coffee bars, and occasionally in my (or the participant's) home. Only one was conducted by telephone. All interviews with Bard staff, actors, Board members, designers, and directors were taped and transcribed with the agreement of the participant. This group totalled almost forty. Once the first draft of the book was completed and edited (May 2016), chapters were presented to Bard for fact-checking and to ascertain if additional information needed to be included.

It was a true delight speaking to members of the "Bard family," who seemed to enjoy the process of being interviewed and reflecting on their experiences. I learned so much and met a wonderful group of people who gave me much more than their time.

In 2017, Bard on the Beach celebrates its twenty-eighth season as one of Canada's largest, not-for-profit professional Shakespeare festivals. It started as an equity co-op, funded primarily by a Canada Council for the Arts exploration grant (awarded to founder and Artistic Director Christopher Gaze in 1990), with a mandate to provide Vancouverites and tourists with affordable, accessible, high-quality Shakespearean productions.

In 1990, six thousand people saw the Company's production of *A Midsummer Night's Dream*, delivered with a budget of $35,000. In 2016, Bard had a budget of over $6 million, and attendance was over 100,000 for the season.

In 1989, Christopher Gaze directed a group of UBC students in *Under Milk Wood* at the Vancouver International Fringe Festival. With the experience of two (unsuccessful) Shakespeare festivals (see Act I), he suggested that this group try a similar venture. So in 1990, with a rented tent and the Canada Council money, the Bard on the Beach dream was born. This is the story of that dream.

As this book concerns an "unconventional" theatre company, its five chapters have been titled as "Acts," each describing an aspect of the background, history, growth, and existence of this unique theatre group.

In Act I, *The Protagonist*, or leading man, is discussed. Christopher Gaze is the face of Bard and, as will be illustrated in the following pages, the reason Bard exists. Act II outlines *The History of Bard on the Beach* through an account of its twenty-eight-year history, much of which was gleaned through reading annual reports as well as through interviews. Act III describes *The Set*, the physical presence of the new permanent office and performance space, as well as the logistics of constructing a temporary theatre in a public park every April and dismantling it in September. Act IV provides information on *The Players*. This is an eclectic collection of managerial and administrative staff who serve behind the scenes to support the actors, designers, directors, and technical crew who, in turn, are supported by a huge pool of volunteers, all of whom work to deliver quality theatre for patrons. Act V, *The Plot Development,* offers information on Bard's significant educational component, an aspect few theatre-goers know about or consider. Finally, the *Epilogue* pulls the story together and provides analysis on why Bard on the Beach is so successful and what the future holds.

I have chosen to use a number of direct quotes (some edited slightly for grammatical reasons) taken from my interviews, as I believe these provide the true, informative, often highly entertaining anecdotes about Bard on the Beach from individuals who have been close to every aspect of the organization. It is their story. My role has been to interpret these words while providing analysis and structure. No financial remuneration was offered or received from Bard for this work. While they granted access, this story of Bard on the Beach is the result of my understanding. If there are mistakes, omissions, or misconceptions, they are entirely mine. ►

Christopher Gaze in England

"Men at some time are masters of their fates. The fault, dear Brutus, is not in our stars, but in ourselves, that we are underlings." JULIUS CAESAR

The PROTAGONIST:

CHRISTOPHER GAZE

I recollect little about my (compulsory) Shakespeare education, which the British education curriculum required all sixteen-year-olds to tackle during the 1970s. What I do remember from these studies is that Shakespeare draws on a number of themes and one of these is "fate." Think about "star-crossed lovers" in Romeo and Juliet. I have always liked the idea of fate—"that consequence yet hanging in the stars" guiding our lives. I like it because it denies personal responsibility. The fact that there could be a God (or gods) playing with my life stipulates that when the wrong decision is made, it is really not my fault. And, likewise, when good things happen, this too is only the result of a higher being responding to my prayers. Of course, this position is juxtaposed with the cliché "You make your own luck." This Act on Christopher Gaze has elements of both trains of thought. As I came to learn more about my protagonist and the direction of his life, I found there were elements of luck, fortune, and fate (being born into his family and the advantage this awarded, together with fortuitous relationships), but also a strong personal drive that had nothing to do with chance and everything to do with his own attributes. The fact that both he and I left our homes in England for Canada at age twenty-three is a coincidence I only learned while researching the book. I also learned we share the same birthday (but I am a lot younger), we both had insecurities about our early educational achievements, and we acknowledge that the career successes in our adopted country would not have been achieved had we not emigrated.

Any discussion about Bard on the Beach cannot be complete without reference to its extremely personable and charismatic leader, Christopher Gaze. This book and the quality of its information can be attributed to the ease with which I gained access to the Bard on the Beach organization through Christopher's championing of the idea. During my initial conversation with Christopher, he suggested I speak to his mother, Joy Gaze (who is three days younger than the Queen of England, and if they went head-to-head on gentility and grace, there would be no clear winner), and sister, Sarah Gaze. Both were heavily involved in the growth and development of Bard and of course were able to offer considerable insights. Christopher joked that they would be able to remember far more than he could. I spoke to both of them for over two hours. This first Act contains their recollections, together with information gained from interviewing Christopher for over four hours and speaking to him on numerous occasions while undertaking the research for this book.

Christopher (according to his mother, nobody calls him Chris, although his father called him Gazey, as does his wife, Jennifer, and friend/colleague Dean Paul Gibson, who calls him that and a number of other "affectionate" terms) was born in Surrey in southern England in 1952 (one year before the Stratford, Ontario, Shakespeare Festival started). His upper middle-class parents owned a medium-sized construction business, which had been in the family for generations, building houses, churches, tennis courts, and then in later years, expanding into furnishings. While Christopher was not pressured to go into the family firm, his mother recalls it was initially presumed, although this presumption was dropped as he demonstrated other, more artistic intentions early on in his childhood. Both his parents had a keen interest in the arts, with his father chair of a local amateur theatre group where his mother was the secretary. Christopher attended Hurstpierpoint College, a traditional English boarding school—which he described as looking like a prison—for ten years, from age eight to eighteen. At this institution, most of the students were encouraged to pursue professional careers as doctors, lawyers, accountants, or administrators. Christopher recalled his first love was always for performance, but

▲ *Christopher Gaze as Ursula in his first Shakespearean production of* Much Ado About Nothing, *1966.*

the school offered a far more traditional and conventional approach to education and did not stage many live productions. Despite few opportunities to pursue his passion, he recalled enjoying school and the few plays that he enthusiastically took advantage of, while acknowledging he did not really thrive there.

According to his mother, Christopher's first acting and theatrical experience was at Horsley Youth Theatre, in the community where he grew up and where she was active in the local amateur theatre. He recalled appearing in reviews put on by his mother "whenever she could have me." In 1966, at the age of fourteen, he undertook his first Shakespeare role at Hurstpierpoint College, as Ursula in *Much Ado About Nothing*. When he was sixteen, he said to his mother, "I'm going to apply to the National Youth Theatre." At that time, about five thousand students applied for acceptance to the prestigious program, which students attended during school holidays and on weekends, in addition to their regular schooling. Christopher gained one of the few places. When asked whether she minded her son becoming an actor, Joy Gaze recalled the sentiments of her husband:

> *Well, my husband was wonderful. He said, "I've given six years of my life for the war [he came out in 1946], and I've fought for freedom, freedom for any future children I had." Christopher kept saying he wanted to be an actor,*

so eventually my husband said, "Look, you've got birthday and Christmas money, I know you'll have to pay for auditions . . . you pay for those auditions and if you get in, your mother and I will support you always. If you don't, you must buckle down and do acting as an amateur," and we all agreed.

Joy Gaze elaborated that while Christopher was totally supportive of this, as it was more than he'd hoped for, a number of her friends and friends of the family "thought we were mad." They were sure Christopher would become like all other "starving actors" and suggested he pursue a more secure and traditional career path.

In the summer of 1968, at age sixteen, Christopher gained a place in the National Youth Theatre (NYT). In the NYT he was with students who shared his passions and interests, in contrast to Hurstpierpoint College. His first international performance occurred that summer. While in rehearsals for *Macbeth*, he was asked to join a tour staging *A Midsummer Night's Dream* in Europe. He did so, but without a speaking part. Upon hearing that his parents were coming to see him in Amsterdam, he managed to secure one line from a fellow actor: "I will, my Lord." This was the first time he spoke Shakespeare on an international stage.

At age eighteen, he decided to apply to theatre schools, including the Bristol Old Vic Theatre School. His mother readily recalled the process:

Bristol offered him an audition over a weekend in school time, so I had to get permission from the school for him to leave. He had to go there by train. He was given a twelve-line poem to memorize on Friday night to recite on Saturday morning. They had classes Friday night. He may not remember, he doesn't remember a lot about all this. He was there all day Saturday, all day Sunday, and left on Monday. I picked him up and drove him to school. I think it was Wednesday morning we had a phone call saying they had accepted him in the eighteen- to twenty-one-year-old class. He was just eighteen. He would do three years, and there were only nine students accepted. And that's how he went to Bristol. We were thrilled that he had made it.

The Bristol Old Vic Theatre School trained actors such as Anthony Hopkins, Jeremy Irons, and Peter Postlethwaite, who was later nominated for an Academy Award (and who apparently spent more than one night sleeping off an alcohol-filled evening on Christopher's bedroom floor while both were studying their art). During his time at Bristol, Christopher received a classical training and opportunity to hone his craft. He remembered being very happy at this time in his life.

In 1973, aged twenty-one, he auditioned for the Theatre North company for a man named Douglas Campbell. This meeting was the start of a lifelong friend-ship and admiration. Campbell was to have an enormous effect on his life and, by default, on Bard on the Beach. He was good at achieving a rapport with younger actors, and over time a familiar father/son bond was created and borne out. After a number of years, they shared holidays together and became very, very close. A copy of a letter Campbell sent to him in 1973 is framed in Christopher's office. Their bond lasted until Campbell died in 2009. As Christopher explained:

He was intimidating but thrilling to be around. You knew you were in the company of somebody extraordinary and, as I say, I was not alone. You can talk to thousands of people who would say the same about him. After only six to eight weeks, he invited me over and I spent a night, obviously in the local pub, then in the farmhouse that he rented and I slept the night . . . I believe Douglas saw in me the potential for someone who could really do something in the theatre. I don't know how he spotted it, but I know what talent-spotting and gold-mining is all about in the arts, and he saw that in me.

Christopher recalled Campbell as a man who was easy to follow and to be influenced by, but their social class backgrounds (Campbell was the son of a postal worker with working-class roots) meant they had to "dance around each other." Campbell offered him his first position in

his theatre company in Sheffield, a city in the north of England, as an actor/assistant stage manager for eighteen pounds (about CAN$30) a week. He played a number of roles in this company and became even better friends with Campbell, despite their different backgrounds: "I was a bit of a toff, and he wasn't, but there was something about him, there was something about him—that's what friendship is, isn't it?"

Once Christopher's contract came to an end, Campbell, who had spent time in Canada as one of the original actors at the Stratford Festival (having been introduced to it by one of its founders, Sir Tyrone Guthrie), encouraged Christopher to cross the Atlantic. Campbell advised him to seek challenges in Canada and not stay in England as they would "stick him in a box," and suggested there were far more opportunities in Canada for an adventurer. "Douglas said to me, 'Look, you've done marvellously with us, but you need to leave here now and get out into the world,'" recalled Christopher. "He was a rebellious, left-wing man; I'm not, I'm much more conservative, out of a blue-blood family, but he, he thought he could show me—if I found myself in other situations, and by his own explanation of life and living—there was another side to life . . . a much more open and liberal view of the world, instead of the strictures of the English class-based society."

Christopher Gaze in Canada

"What country, friends, is this?"
TWELFTH NIGHT

The day after receiving Campbell's advice, at the age of twenty-three, Christopher told his parents he was leaving to go to live in Canada, despite having had an audition with the highly prestigious Royal Shakespeare Company and a job offer at a theatre in Nairobi. He booked a passage on a ship, named the *Stefan Batory*, which sailed from the Port of London to Montreal.

Joy Gaze acknowledged the tremendous influence Campbell had on her son: "He really loved Douglas, I think; he looked on him as a father figure." Before Christopher left England, Campbell wrote six letters of introduction on blue airmail paper to six influential individuals he knew in Canada who would help his prodigy build a career. Christopher left England on May 14, 1975, for a country that was just beginning to wake up to the joys of Shakespeare. His mother recalled the early days of this life-changing trip:

> When he landed at Montreal and said, *"I'm an actor; I've come here to work,"* he was greeted with, *"We don't want any British actors, thank you."* He didn't have any paperwork. Douglas Campbell would not have thought about it, as he'd been backwards and forwards to Canada since the 1950s, before there was any paperwork . . . He [Christopher] wasn't going back to England, as he'd just got there, so he used his contacts from Douglas.

Christopher drew on Campbell's first contact and went to stay in Toronto with Bruno Gerussi, the famous Canadian actor best known for his leading role in the CBC television series *The Beachcombers*. Following a few days in that city, he moved on to Stratford, using another of Campbell's letters of introduction to stay with Bill Needles, one of Canada's best-known Shakespearean actors and one of the founding company members of the Stratford Festival. While he was there, it soon became apparent that to be able to work in Canada, he needed to obtain his landed immigrant status. For this to be granted, it was necessary to leave the country. Bill Needles's sister-in-law had relatives who owned ranches in Montana. They offered unpaid employment, but free room and board. So Christopher moved to Montana and became a ranch hand for the summer of 1975. His brief time in Montana and Wyoming was not without acting experience; his sister recounted one occasion when he was asked to play the role of a butler for a senator who was having a dinner party and wanted to impress his guests.

Another contact from Campbell was Christopher Newton, who at the time was the Artistic Director at the Vancouver Playhouse. While in Montana, Christopher contacted him and Newton agreed to place an advertisement for an actor with unique attributes. By showing the immigration authorities that no one in Canada had these qualifications, Newton was then able to offer the position to Christopher. As the latter explained:

I started the immigration process from Minneapolis [which was the nearest office that accepted applications], and Newton had to prove no one else could do what he wanted done. So he placed an advertisement that read: "Wanted: classically trained English young actor." When he got no takers, he could say to immigration, "Look, my boy is there." Then I got landed immigrant status. They stamped my passport October 9, 1975, in Vancouver, and subsequently I became a citizen.

Newton gave him a job that started in January 1976. Upon arriving in Vancouver in the fall of 1975, Christopher had to look for work. He described arriving with few resources and too much pride to telephone his family requesting money. He started to look for employment, but also telephoned Bruno Gerussi, who was working in British Columbia, to say he was in Vancouver. He explained that he was looking for work and somewhere to live. Later that day, he found that $400 had been deposited in his bank account from Bruno, money not sought but much needed at that time.

Christopher described arriving in Vancouver and "hitting the ground running." Early days involved living in a rather seedy apartment where the rent was cheap and initially taking work in a restaurant, but he quickly moved on to find work within his profession, undertaking contracts for the CBC and then replacing an actor in a revue called *Beyond the Fringe*.

I arrived in Vancouver and had sixty dollars and thought, "What on earth am I going to do?" Move wood, paint a wall? But then I started to get jobs because I was desirable, frankly. I know what it's like as an Artistic Director now—you are looking for talented young men and women like I was, well trained, and that was the hardest thing to find.

While in Toronto, staying with Bruno Gerussi, Christopher had made a video audition for the CBC. In December, his phone rang and it was the casting director for CBC who wanted him to audition for a TV drama called *Ladies in Retirement* in Toronto. He explained he was in a show in Vancouver, so they offered to fly him out on his day off and pay the expenses. "So I went to Toronto, got the job, finished the contract in Vancouver, and left... to spend Christmas 1975 in Stratford."

This job was well paid, but accepting it was not without headaches. Christopher described the commitment he had to Newton, the man who had been instrumental in helping him gain landed immigrant status and the ability to work in Canada:

Christopher Newton was so gracious and did the heavy lifting and got me into Canada. I went to see him and thank him my very first day in Vancouver. The Playhouse offices were on Beatty Street in those days. Over the next while, I volunteered for the Playhouse and helped them move into an alfresco studio theatre on Robson Street. Christopher offered me a job in a production of Macbeth *that they were going to do at the Vancouver Playhouse in January—I was to play the Third Witch! Meanwhile, I was getting work on CBC Radio and at City Stage. Then I was offered a wonderful role for CBC TV in Toronto, and when I told Chris, he asked me what I wanted to do. It was a professional dilemma... I replied that I would like to take the TV drama in Toronto. He took it very badly and subsequently never engaged me again. Over the years, as an Artistic Director, there have been many instances when actors have opted to accept contracts that they thought were more potent than Bard's. I let them go and wish them well. It is part of the theatre business, and I strive to do all I can to further actors' opportunities. In spite of everything, I will always remain indebted to Christopher Newton for getting me into Canada.*

After the television show, Christopher Gaze auditioned for the Shaw Festival and worked there in 1976, 1977, and 1979. When describing these times, Christopher became quite animated and entertaining, relaying numerous highly amusing anecdotes (often featuring women and a young Englishman's love life). These would make a highly entertaining read should they ever appear in a Christopher Gaze memoir (which he does have ambitions to write), but which, I suspect, would be cut from a story about Bard on the Beach. Nevertheless, one Board member suggested Christopher's past love life could form an appendix in itself, while another interviewee commented, "Christopher is very willing to talk about his love life, and when he has done with that, he wants to know all about yours."

A couple of the more lively tales Christopher recounted include meeting George Bush Sr. and Katharine Hepburn through an actress almost twice his age with whom he was having an affair. He described her as "one of the great Canadian actresses at the time, who had all her demons." The Mrs. Robinson parallel was not lost on him, although at this point in the interview all I could think of was a quote from Othello, who described himself as "one that lov'd not wisely but too well." It was obviously a very entertaining summer both on and off stage. During this period in our conversation, no information about professional, artistic, or career development was offered, only recollections about the newly arrived, young, good-looking immigrant with a very sexy, smooth, sultry English accent and his love life. When the daughter of his seductress told her he had been seeing other women, she promptly hit him, thus putting an end to what he called a "lively summer." As he described it, "During the summer of 1976, I had lots of girlfriends, I'd been engaged, I was always trying to get married to anybody. I don't know why, I'd just fall in love and wanted to get married."

In 1978 he took time away from Shaw to put on his own dinner show entitled *A Little of What You Fancy*, which he described as being similar to English musical theatre. The show ran for three months under Christopher's leadership, in an Italian restaurant called Armando's in Toronto. After he left, the show continued for five months. This was the first time he had organized his own theatre.

Christopher described this period of existence as a virtually carefree and happy young actor: "I just went from contract to contract. I was always fearful of not having work, but I was footloose and fancy-free, didn't have to leave a wife and children—I didn't even have an address; I just lived where I worked."

During the summer of 1978, he learned a man named Peter Coe was in Toronto.

This famous English director, who had just completed directing *Oliver!* on the London stage, for which he received considerable acclaim, was about to take up the position as Artistic Director at the Citadel Theatre in Edmonton. Christopher described going to his hotel in Toronto, finding which room he was staying in, and knocking on his door: "He let me in and by time I got out, he'd hired me."

So after three years in eastern Canada, in the fall of 1978, he moved to Edmonton and not only gained work at the Citadel with Peter Coe but was also employed at the Northern Light Theatre company doing lunchtime theatre. It was during this time that he met the woman who would later become his first wife, Merrilyn Gann. He recalled the day during rehearsal when she sidled up to him and said, "Would you like to have an affair with me?" It was "just about the most exciting thing I'd ever heard in my life. I wasn't a sophisticated lover, and in the past I wasn't able to deal with these types of requests. That's how we met."

After the contract in Edmonton finished in early April 1979, he returned to Shaw. It was during a party in 1979 that Christopher ran into his mentor, Douglas Campbell, again. "He put his arm around my shoulder and said, 'Ah Christopher, we're going to do something, aren't we.' I didn't know what, but I did know it was a quiet, gentle inspiration from someone I loved very, very much."

In 1979, while at Shaw, a director asked Christopher for recommendations for strong women to cast, so he suggested Merrilyn, having spent considerable time with her in Edmonton. She was hired, and by the end of the summer they were, as he described, "a fixture." They were married within a year. In 1980, Christopher and Merrilyn moved back to Edmonton, joined Northern Light Theatre, and started to play regularly at the Citadel Theatre. They purchased a house in Edmonton, and their two sons were born there—Joshua in 1981 and Zachary in 1983.

In Edmonton in 1980, Northern Light Theatre initiated a Shakespeare Festival, which Christopher was heavily involved with, that operated from a simple tent on Connors Hill, where the audience sat on blankets. It was successful in its first year, expanded rapidly in its second season, and then collapsed, losing a considerable amount of money. Christopher described being part of several festivals that went sideways in fairly quick succession. "Northern Light managed to continue after 1981, but they had to stop doing Shakespeare in the tent in the summertime because they lost too much money. Scott Swan became Artistic Director of Lennoxville Festival [in Quebec], and we all went out there in 1982. Halfway through that summer, it went broke and we all went home." In retrospect, although disappointing, this early introduction to Shakespeare festivals was a vital learning process for our young protagonist.

Christopher disliked living in Edmonton. In the winter, he would ask himself, "What am I doing here? What is mankind doing here?" In spring 1983 the family decided to move to Vancouver to be nearer Merrilyn's parents. So Vancouver became home, and "fate" continued to happen: "Literally, as we moved into our house, the phone rang and it was a couple of people who were starting a Shakespeare Festival in Vancouver in a tent in Vanier Park." They asked if Christopher wanted to play leading roles, two of which he'd played in Edmonton with Northern Light. So he did the summer of 1983, which was quite successful, but they expanded too quickly and went out of business by the beginning of August 1984. He was playing Richard III at the time.

The same scenario happened with the Vancouver Shakespeare Festival as had occurred in Edmonton. Here again, the Company had a successful first year, then expanded too quickly and faced unforeseen circumstances in the second year, including a newspaper strike that restricted advertising and reviews, a bus strike, and bad weather, all of which meant having to close ahead of schedule, in early August. These two Shakespeare festivals both suffered from similar fates: rapid expansion and financial insecurities. Business analysts and commerce academics often observe many small business owners failing two or three times before identifying the right niche and operating a business that then succeeds. It would prove to be invaluable experience for Christopher.

Then in 1988, Christopher's father died, at age sixty-eight, of pancreatic cancer. He described this as the most profound thing that ever happened to him, and recounted his father's visit from the UK to Vancouver in October 1987 for his son Josh's sixth birthday:

*He came on his own, without my mother, which was unusual. He knew he wasn't well, and I could sense that something very serious was wrong with him. He stayed for a couple of weeks. I was in a play at the Arts Club on Seymour Street at the time—*The Mystery of Irma Vep. *We used to go on walks in the day, and he would come and see the show in the evening. It was as if we knew that his life was in the balance and we wanted to embrace every moment together. There is no question that in a very British sort of way, our father/son relationship was impeccable. His love for me and my love for him resound inside me every moment of my life. One day, we went to see a performance of* A Midsummer Night's Dream *at the Vancouver Playhouse. Dad turned to me at the end and said quietly, "You can do better than that, can't you, Gazey?" His intuition was like Douglas Campbell's—they both had extraordinary faith in me and believed that I had the right stuff to do something visionary and worthwhile with my life. Over the next ten months, I travelled backwards and forwards to the UK as my father's health declined. And then he died . . . I knew I would never see his like again. After I got over the initial grief, I began to wake up to what my mission was in life. Dad's death had given me the fire to take control of my destiny, to not be at the whimsy of casting directors and therefore to "do something!" I was in my mid-thirties and ready to try a different direction. One evening, filled with my father-in-law's blackberry wine, I chatted to him about my life as an actor. He was, in essence, a working man and didn't understand the dedication and passion of an actor, so he suggested that I was "flogging a dead horse" with my life in the theatre! "Flogging a dead horse?" I thought, "No, I'm bloody well not!" So the next day, with a clear head, I knew my mission. I was ready. And I started to talk about the idea of a Shakespeare festival in Vancouver once again.*

The Birth of an Idea

*"Our doubts are traitors, And make
us lose the good we oft might win,
By fearing to attempt."*

MEASURE FOR MEASURE

I n 1989, Christopher was approached by a group of University of British Columbia students with an interesting invitation: to direct a group of graduate students from UBC in a Vancouver Fringe Festival production of *Under Milk Wood*.

I had not been involved in productions like this before—theatre co-ops—but essentially everyone provides what they can financially to pay for the show, and then you get paid back from the box office revenues, if there are any! Anyway, we did it and it was all great fun. I enjoyed the camaraderie, and the group had an exciting dynamic. We performed on Main Street in Vancouver and then took it to Presentation House in North Vancouver. One evening, sitting in the Fringe Bar on Main Street, I told the group of my idea to begin a Shakespeare festival in Vancouver, and there was a huge amount of enthusiasm . . . this was the critical moment that Bard began. All through the rest

of '89 and the early part of 1990, we planned, gradually attracting other forces to help us.

This planning process was augmented by a family holiday in May 1990. Christopher, his mother, and his sister, Sarah, travelled to Bangkok. Sarah was finishing her time in Hong Kong where she had been living and working. "It was really the first time we had all been together since my father had died," recalled Christopher, "so there was a piquancy and sense of loss as we toured around." Joy Gaze remembered this family holiday well:

Christopher was going to begin the project Bard on the Beach when he got back to Canada, so as we toured around, we talked about it all endlessly! He had talked of starting his own company for years, ever since his Shaw Festival days, but we didn't take him very seriously. Now we saw something new in him and so we all poured out all our ideas as we drove through Malaysia. Christopher was driving, and Sarah scribbled down notes as I followed the map. It was an amazing time—we seemed to talk of little else except this summer project that he was about to embark on. All the different aspects of producing Bard came to the fore, and his direction of A Midsummer Night's Dream. Our adventure together helped Christopher form many seminal ideas for what was about "to be"!

In analyzing Bard on the Beach as an amazingly successful business, it's imperative to understand how Christopher's family background and upbringing, which involved an understanding of business, helped Bard to grow and succeed where so many similar theatre companies have failed. His mother provided an understanding of this inherited knowledge when she recalled a younger Christopher:

> *My husband talked business all the time to him…At the dinner table when he was five and six and seven, he'd be listening, and he always preferred as a little boy to be with older people, especially men. He'd listen very carefully to what they were talking about. My husband, Douglas, always used to say to him, "If you ever start a business [no one ever thought he would], you must make sure your foundation is firm and solid. Just because you are successful one year, don't go and build up an enormous place. Make sure the foundation is there; go slowly, go very, very slowly." And that is what he's done.*

Christopher's family background coupled with his first-hand experience of two initially successful and then failed attempts at establishing Shakespeare festivals in Western Canada ensured that when he brainstormed and developed the concept of his own, it was done in a slow, practical, fiscally sound way. His training as a classical actor at one of the world's greatest theatre schools ensured he had the formal education and knowledge of his craft. These three elements—business acumen, formal artistic training, and first-hand practical experience of Shakespeare festival companies—created the perfect combination of learned experiences leading to his founding of Bard on the Beach in 1990.

But it is not just these learned traits and experiences that matter. There were also fortuitous events—the "fate factor." If he had not met Douglas Campbell, would he have chosen to launch his career in Canada? Had Campbell not given him the six letters of introduction to some very influential individuals working in the arts, would he have been successful in gaining work in Canada and acquiring his landed immigrant status? Had he not met certain directors at certain times in his career, he may not have been exposed to Shakespeare festivals and learned from them. And if he had fallen passionately for the older lover who seduced him at the Shaw Festival in the late seventies, and decided to be faithful to her at the tender age of twenty-three, where would Christopher Gaze be today?

◄ *Christopher studying* King Lear.

The Man Today

"What fates impose, that men must needs abide." HENRY VI, PART THREE

Any student of politics knows there is a wealth of literature on charismatic leaders and how they shaped nations (e.g., Winston Churchill, Pierre Elliott Trudeau, Nelson Mandela, Martin Luther King). Commerce students are also taught that the success of some businesses in creating a unique organizational culture is the direct result of the personalities and commitments of their founders: e.g., Richard Branson (Virgin), Howard Schultz (Starbucks), Bill Gates (Microsoft), Henry Ford (Ford Motor Company). In the field of sports and entertainment, there are individuals who also spring to mind—Wayne Gretzky, Steve Nash, Oprah Winfrey. These individuals not only have a unique charismatic personality, they also possess a deep understanding of their market, their customers, and a passion for their product.

Charismatic is a term frequently used by those who know Christopher. As one Board member shared, "He has this wonderful charisma, and he's so easygoing, and he never fails to compliment when compliments are due, and you feel so highly appreciative of what others have done. He's just wonderful to work with." Another observed, "Christopher is gracious; yes, he's a gracious person and he's charismatic, and I say that in the most positive way, not in a negative way. Christopher is Bard."

The Bard on the Beach website describes Christopher as an "extremely talented actor and director" with a "four-decade professional acting career" who has "performed locally…as well as in virtually every major centre across Canada, England and the United States." In addition, he frequently performs in and directs Bard productions; is involved in a number of other art organizations such as the Vancouver Symphony, Chor Leoni, and Knowledge Network; is a member of the Order of British Columbia; and holds two honorary doctorate degrees. While informative, these descriptions fail to paint the true picture of Christopher Gaze. This is where my own experience and that of my respondents comes in.

Living in Vancouver for over twenty-five years has meant I have always known of Christopher Gaze. I cannot remember when I first encountered him, or why; I just know that since moving here, there have been certain dependable things: Stanley Park, the rain, the North Shore Mountains, raccoons, congestion on the Lions Gate Bridge (and debates about what to do about it), and Christopher Gaze. While politicians and city mayors change, Christopher has remained. Not only is he the face and advocate for Bard, but he is frequently on CBC and other media outlets discussing some aspect of the arts.

Many who are associated with him commented on the fact that he is synonymous with Bard. As one designer put it, "What other theatre company has such a visible head? He is the brand, the best spokesperson, and he's so charming to everyone who knows him. He represents the Company to the community. He kind of is Bard on the Beach."

A Board member agreed: "Christopher *is* Bard. Bard is Christopher. He is the heartbeat of Bard and, man, he is just on all the time. He's working even when he is not working, 24/7, 365. He's amazing. He says 'thank you' to me all the time, and I say, 'Christopher, if you ever want to thank me, come over to my house around 8 PM and read bedtime stories to my children.' With that voice and, you know, the way he is—the velvety voice."

One actor described Christopher as "very comfortable in the public eye . . . always on the radio and doing public appearances and all that kind of stuff. It's part of his background as an actor; he is very comfortable about being the public face of the Company."

I have encountered him in other theatres when we were both audience members, and seen him in the liquor store, and riding his bike. I've switched on the TV to find him on Knowledge Network. Last year, I encountered him on the field-hockey pitch playing for the Vancouver Grey Hawks, along with my spouse and a number of other men of a certain age. A few years ago, I had dinner with him and his wife through mutual friends at the Vancouver Tennis Club.

On the Bard stage, introducing plays, he always seems to be acknowledging and waving to members of the audience he recognizes. He is able to make you feel part of the Company, not just a member of the audience who needs to turn off a cell phone. Prior to the performances, he is seen wandering around the Bard Village, talking to volunteers and patrons, mingling and enthusing over what we are about to see. It is difficult to imagine whether Bard would have reached the success it sees today without this gentleman.

Another Board member agreed: "I can sum up, because we have become very good friends over the years, that he is a human being who has prodigious talents, an amazing skill set, a huge presence, with that a big ego—and everything that's positive about the term 'ego.' And yet, at the same time, he can be completely humble and open and respectful of everyone. For me, that is the ultimate in self-confidence, to be able to be that open."

When speaking to another Board member about the future of Bard, I asked what would happen if Christopher got run over by a bus. His jaw dropped, his

TOP AND RIGHT ‹ The Comedy of Errors, *2015.*

BOTTOM LEFT ‹ *Christopher and Vancouver mayor Gregor Robertson.*

eyes widened and watered, and he slowly and sincerely told me that no bus driver in Vancouver would ever, ever run over Christopher Gaze and I should banish such disturbing thoughts from my mind immediately. Yet another Board member quipped that if Christopher were abducted by aliens, he would start Shakespeare in Space, and it would be a huge success, as all the Martians would fall in love with him (as Vancouverites have) and sponsor the productions. I could fill a book with only the positive comments and admiration everyone associated with Bard has for this man.

Many of the comments are about his unbridled enthusiasm. As a member of Bard management said, "The fact is we are very much founder-driven. I think Christopher is very much still so present and enthused, and very much a driving force within the organization. It's so special, and I don't know where he gets his enthusiasm—and enthusiasm after twenty-eight years is the key. I find that astonishing, and it's a huge part of the Company's success. He's been 'President Enthusiastic' for twenty-eight years."

An actor echoed, "Could it have gotten as big without him? Well, there is no denying that his enthusiasm for the work and for the Company is really unmatchable. He's so tireless and committed to keeping this thing going, and he does it in a way that is very different from other artistic producers in Vancouver, certainly in this city. He is such an incredible face for the Company; people associate him with this Company so closely."

During the course of the interviews, I was expecting someone might say something negative about Christopher Gaze—not necessarily nasty, but just a flaw in his character, a trait we all have, part of being human. After months of research, the only one that emerged in over one hundred hours of taped discussion with more than forty individuals is barely worth inclusion. One person told me, after a period of considerable reflection, and after I pressured him to reveal any character flaws, that Christopher Gaze cheats at golf. But doesn't everyone? I imagine that cynical readers and skeptics may think I received considerable payment from Christopher or the Bard enterprise for offering such a glowing interpretation of my protagonist. They may surmise that I obviously did not search long or hard enough to uncover "the real dirt" to taint such a rose-coloured interpretation. But the truth is, everyone I spoke to loves Christopher Gaze.

CLOCKWISE FROM TOP LEFT

1 ➤ *Christopher opens the BMO Mainstage, June 2011.*

2 ➤ PHOTO BY YUKIKO ONLEY.

3 ➤ PHOTO BY ALEX WATERHOUSE-HAYWARD.

4 ➤ *Christopher in the Village, 2010.*

To further my attempts to find the "real" story, I arranged to speak to his wife, Jennifer, who has of course known him for many years and who I felt sure would be able to tell me the truth, as only a woman who has lived with a man for a considerable period of time can. Surely, she would be able to paint the accurate picture and illustrate all those character flaws his friends and colleagues were unable or unwilling to supply. After consideration, she shared with me the following:

> I call him Gazey, and I'm going to write a book. It's going to be called, Waiting for Gazey. *Christopher doesn't have fast-forward. Christopher doesn't have a fast speed. Christopher always thinks he has more time than he does, so he's rushing out at the last minute to get to something he's supposed to get to. So if there is a flaw, it's managing his time. He gets a lot accomplished, but I can see it coming: he's not dressed, he's looking at his computer, and I'm thinking, "He has to get to the office at 9:00 and he's riding his bike; he's never going to get there."*

Jennifer Gaze went on to praise her husband of over fifteen years (as he always does her, even in her absence at public gatherings), but also talked of having to share him, of walking along and expecting him to be at her side, but finding he's stopped to talk to another person he knows, or of going out for a quiet dinner but encountering others who want to engage him. "And if there is a flaw, it's not a real flaw: his whole family has to share him. We have to share him. We don't get him 100 percent. We maybe get him 40 percent, and I'm talking about his children and grandchildren."

The benefits of birth, fate, and circumstances, combined with his innate energy, enthusiasm, charismatic personality, and an ability to convey this to others and actively engage them to commit to his dream has resulted in the success of Bard on the Beach we see today. It would seem no one in Vancouver, or the broader arts community in Canada, does not know of him and his accomplishments with Bard on the Beach. However, it seems that a few years ago, while attending the Stratford Shakespeare Festival in Ontario, Christopher encountered someone who was unaware of his accomplishments. As the Board member accompanying him said,

You can't go anywhere in Stratford without someone coming up to him and really loving him and loving what he's done… We saw a number of amazing plays and Margaret Atwood was there, and I am a Margaret Atwood fan. She is amazing. So Christopher goes up to her in the intermission and says, "Hello, I'm Christopher Gaze," and she completely blew him off— she didn't know who he was. And, of course, people come up to him all the time, but to her, he was just another person, and it was just so funny to see. In Vancouver everyone knows who he is, and it was so funny to see Christopher actually had someone who didn't know and didn't care who he was.

Clearly, if one of Canada's leading authors doesn't know about him, or Bard on the Beach, there is still more for Christopher Gaze to do and achieve. ►

ACT II

"*Such stuff as dreams are made on.*"

THE TEMPEST

The HISTORY *of*
BARD ON
THE BEACH:

THE SEVEN AGES OF A
THEATRE COMPANY

One of my favourite speeches in Shakespeare is from *As You Like It*. I use the first line for the title of this book and have organized this Act to parallel the "seven ages" described. Here is the entire monologue, as delivered by sad Jaques:

All the world's a stage,
And all the men and women merely players;
They have their exits and their entrances,
And one man in his time plays many parts,
His acts being seven ages. At first the infant,
Mewling and puking in the nurse's arms.
And then, the whining school-boy with his satchel
And shining morning face, creeping like snail
Unwillingly to school. And then the lover,
Sighing like furnace, with a woeful ballad
Made to his mistress' eyebrow. Then a soldier,
Full of strange oaths, and bearded like the pard,
Jealous in honour, sudden and quick in quarrel,
Seeking the bubble reputation
Even in the cannon's mouth. And then the justice,
In fair round belly with good capon lin'd,
With eyes severe, and beard of formal cut,
Full of wise saws and modern instances;
And so he plays his part. The sixth age shifts
Into the lean and slipper'd pantaloon,
With spectacles on nose and pouch on side,
His youthful hose well sav'd, a world too wide
For his shrunk shank; and his big manly voice,
Turning again toward childish treble, pipes
And whistles in his sound. Last scene of all,
That ends this strange eventful history,
Is second childishness and mere oblivion,
Sans teeth, sans eyes, sans taste, sans
    everything.

While it seemed fitting to draw upon these stages to add context to the twenty-eight years of Bard, the final corpse stage is clearly not applicable. Bard is anything but dead. I therefore seriously struggled with the decision to use this template to structure the organization's history. In the end, after discussions with Christopher and Claire, we decided it did provide a wonderful structure for the second act in the story of this unique theatre company.

The Birth of Bard on the Beach: 1989–1990

(The Infant)

"You know not what you do."

JULIUS CAESAR

"In the beginning, Bard was just a group of people," one Bard actor/director said. As we learned in Act I, Christopher Gaze advanced the idea of creating a Shakespeare festival in Vancouver to a group of UBC theatre graduate students in fall 1989. He recalled their enthusiasm as he outlined his vision: "They all said, 'Oh yes!' Remember, I was the older theatre professional—I was thirty-seven—and they were about twenty-two and beginning their professional lives. But they were great! I told them we needed a tent in a Vancouver park, and it needed to be open at one end . . . In Edmonton in 1980/81, it was open at one end, and in Vancouver in 1983/84, it was closed. I believed it was vital to open the tent and frame the glorious backdrop we have here in Vancouver."

During this period, he not only discussed the venture with his mother, sister, and former wife, all of whom were very supportive, but brainstormed with others in his community, including his children's teacher:

I remember talking about it to a lot of people. People come up to me now and say, "Remember we had that conversation and you said you wanted to get something going?" One time when I dropped the children off at their Montessori school, I chatted with a super teacher called Rhonda Munro, who encouraged me to get on with the idea of this new theatre company that I was endlessly talking about! I thank her for her encouragement.

In October, November, and December 1989, Christopher and the original group worked tirelessly to get their concept established. While Christopher acknowledged his passion for the idea, he credits the group's enthusiasm and proactive organizing of meetings, describing some of the students as being "all over the idea" and looking for something to sink their teeth into. One of the original group recalled it as a thrilling time, but cautioned that if they had given serious consideration to how likely it was not to succeed, they might never have gone ahead. But despite the fact they were all young and "didn't have a clue" how to run a theatre, they just did it, with a real sense of group responsibility. As one actor described, "In the early days, I wrote the application for a grant, I wrote the press release and did the society's registration, and we had never done this thing before; we just had to do it."

At the same time, Christopher was equally excited and committed to the initiative he felt sure would be successful. As he wrote in his 1993 submission to the Board, his vision was simple: he believed that people would come if his group could produce Shakespeare "in an affordable and accessible manner, in a location that British Columbians would find irresistible on a warm summer's evening."

The last time a Shakespeare Festival had been attempted in Vancouver, it had been in Vanier Park by the water, but Christopher doubted that the Park Board would allow them to do it there again. So when he approached the government officials, he asked for a location away from Vanier Park, at Spanish Banks near the volleyball courts. But the Park Board suggested the festival be located at Vanier Park, which was in his eyes a far superior location. He accepted their suggestion, along with an offer of an alcohol licence, an initiative that failed. He let the alcohol licence lapse for a few years, laughingly acknowledging that Vancouver audiences needed a slow, steady introduction to not only the appreciation of Shakespeare but the enjoyment of alcohol outside while partaking in theatre. Bard is now one of the few venues to allow the consumption of alcohol in the theatre during performances. When the seating for the latest tent was being discussed in 2010, cup holders were specified to the supplier by Bard administration, illustrating their willingness to be different and to understand their customers' wants.

The initial group named themselves the Full House Theatre Company, and Bard on the Beach was the project, with the first performance being *A Midsummer Night's Dream*. At that time, there was no money, so an application for a Canada Council exploratory grant was made. They received $18,000.

Christopher recalled phoning Canada Council from a payphone in the departure lounge prior to a flight to Hong Kong and being told that they were going to receive a Canada Council Explorations Grant to explore the idea. "The young actors that had been a part of our *Under Milk Wood* production were first-class in fundraising, and especially at grant writing. They had used my name when we applied to Canada Council, and it worked. It was a sensible and wise move, as I was the artist with a professional track record. Anyway, this was the money that put us over the top, and it all went to the project that we were now calling Bard on the Beach!"

Christopher was quick to recall the names of a few individuals who were early contributors to the project: "We finally raised $35,000 from all sorts of different sources. A wonderful cheque came from one of our co-op member's stepfather—her name was Corinne Hebden, and she played Hermia in *Dream*. He generously gave us $6,000. We had a fundraising dinner at the Alma Street Café. Hugh Pickett and David Y.H. Lui emceed the event! Great names from the past who all stepped up. More money was raised at garage sales and donations from family and friends, people in the co-op, and anyone we could find!"

Christopher discovered he had a facility for fundraising and enjoyed it. In interviews with members of the current Bard fundraising committee, this skill as an extremely talented fundraiser was mentioned repeatedly. He attributed it to the fact that he'd "always been an organizing sort of person. I liked to put on things and make things happen . . . I have always had a bit of a feel for it." He recalled a time at theatre school when he was only about nineteen and organized a whole trip for the school to go to Stratford-upon-Avon, including renting a coach and buying the theatre tickets. A Board member quipped that Christopher could have been a multi-millionaire by now if he had chosen to be a stock promoter, because of his interpersonal skills and his almost innate ability to sell. Many Vancouverites and Bard lovers, myself included, believe he did, however, make the right career choice.

Interestingly, there seems to be no firm answer to the question of who came up with the name "Bard on the Beach." The leading contender seems to be Laura White, an original member of the co-op, who may now be employed as a nurse in Vancouver. Christopher and a couple of members of the original group believe it to be Laura, but after such a long period of time, memories fade and no one knows for sure.

In addition to obtaining funding, the group had to create a Board that included a

▲ *Humble beginnings: the Bard on the Beach tent in its inaugural season, 1990.*

president, treasurer, and secretary. Again, Christopher's fortuitous encounters came into play. During his search, he sat beside a woman at a Presentation House Theatre production who seemed to know of him. When he told her he was starting a theatre company to bring Shakespeare to Vancouver, she expressed interest. "So I started to see Valerie Thoem," recalled Christopher, "and she was active in the Liberal Party and had friends who got involved, but in particular the great force that was Grant Burnyeat." Grant was a lawyer who subsequently became the first president of Bard on the Beach and to this day maintains a keen interest and is a strong supporter. In addition to Grant Burnyeat and Valerie Thoem, Donna Reid (later Donner Celle), Judy

Stevens, and Betty Chan were active as the first community Board members.

So Bard on the Beach began as an equity co-op in the summer of 1990 with ten founding members (see Appendices). Rehearsals took place at the Vancouver Playhouse. The first production on July 22, 1990, was *A Midsummer Night's Dream*. Tickets were $7.50 (the price of a movie ticket) and the season lasted five weeks, with a total of thirty-four performances taking place that summer in a tent that accommodated 275.

"This was a first for a lot of us, such a big venture, we didn't know if it would

48

work," one actor recalled. "We were putting up this tent in the middle of the park, hoping people would come, and we were all so young, the core group; Christopher was the oldest." Many things illustrate just how "fly by the seat of the pants" the whole venture was. For example, the actors in the co-op helped with every aspect of the production, from erecting the tent (which was on loan from the Vancouver Children's Festival), pounding in the tent pegs, and engaging in the physical labour required to construct the venue, to selling tickets, taking telephone orders, and working the concession in costume. Sometimes, when additional seating was required to secure increased revenue, chairs were taken from the dressing room, causing the actors to kneel or stand to apply makeup. The Company's insurance policy required twenty-four-hour security on-site, so each night, one of the male actors was tasked with sleeping on the stage (female actors were not asked to perform this role).

At the end of the first season, the delighted co-operative made some additional money by returning empty pop and juice cans and bottles. "After the show, the two of us and the boys picked up all the cans that were left," recalled Sarah Gaze. "I had collected all the cans for the season—we were penniless, we had no money at Bard, none at all—and Christopher and I took the cans back to the Safeway on Fraser Street and we got $76, and that was gold."

Six thousand people attended the inaugural year, with performances taking place in late July and August. Supportive reviews—the *Vancouver Province* newspaper described it as "Good, old-fashioned, barn-storming Shakespeare"—together with innovative publicity stunts, including one involving the Vancouver Coast Guard and some of the cast on the front page of the *Vancouver Sun* newspaper, created a buzz. As one actor recalled, "We got a lot of press and I don't remember playing to small houses ever. About two hundred people in the audience." Christopher also recognized that patrons would be wooed by an open backdrop, and although the tent was not designed to be open, it was lifted halfway. This singularly insightful act remains a legacy to these early days. All performances on the Mainstage take place against an open backdrop. "We had to test the waters, and the waters were good; everyone loved it," recalled Christopher. To top it all off, 1990 was also the first year the City of Vancouver put on a summer fireworks display, which proved to be a great draw.

One of Bard's current directors recalled his first encounter with Bard, when he went to see *A Midsummer Night's Dream* on the same day as an afternoon performance of *Les Misérables* at the Queen Elizabeth [Theatre]. "Frankly, I was beguiled by *Midsummer,* and I had a better time there than at the touring production of *Les Mis.* The rustic nature, the outdoor thing, it was such a charming evening that so many have discovered over the years."

The first season saw twenty-seven actors paid $1,200 each (expenditure for actors is now over $700,000 annually) and, as mentioned, they all did a lot besides performing. In addition to rehearsals, actors were involved in business meetings, which took place at various abodes and were fit in whenever all were present, to organize the logistics of the festival, such as publicity and promotions. Christopher recalled personally earning about $10,000 total income ($1,200 from the co-op) that first year.

As well, the challenges faced by this young troupe in mounting outdoor performances were compounded when the local vagrant (and frequently intoxicated) population accessed the venue and added additional colour to the productions, a challenge that continues (see Act III).

At the end of the season, the site had to be left as it was found, so volunteers, actors, family, and friends were tasked with searching for and removing every nail, screw, cigarette butt, and anything else left on the grass, to ensure the site could be used again the following year. The same requirement is enforced by the Park Board today.

(see Act III)

[SCENE II]

Moving Forward: 1990–1991
(The Schoolboy)

"Once more unto the breach, dear friends, once more." HENRY V

After the initial success of Bard, the co-operative debated how to move forward. Christopher (and the community Board members), having first-hand experience of Shakespeare festivals in Edmonton and Vancouver and their unfortunate fates (as shown in Act I, both closed in their second season), wanted to develop a traditional, formalized structure consisting of an Artistic Director and Managing Director who were accountable to a Board of Directors. Other members in the Company had alternative views and wanted to continue as a co-operative. Christopher recalled a series of meetings, some combative, leading to one in late October 1990 where someone accused him of wanting to take over the theatre company. "Grant [Burnyeat] could see I was going to rise to it and say something I'd maybe regret. I remember I took a breath and felt his big hand clamping my arm, 'What Christopher wanted to say . . .' He could realize at this point this organization was going to crash and burn."

Although the organization may not have crashed and burned, it did break

TOP ‹ *Laurier Dubeau and Denyse Wilson in* As You Like It, *1991.*

BOTTOM ‹ As You Like It, *1991.*

apart. Five Board members endorsed the traditional business model Christopher wanted, and in December 1990, Bard on the Beach officially registered as a not-for-profit under the Society Act of British Columbia, with Grant Burnyeat agreeing to take on the role as the first president. Other members of the co-operative believed the way forward was to continue as a co-operative, calling itself Full House Theatre Company. This company dissolved a couple of years later.

In articulating the factors leading up to the division, Christopher explained that part of the complexity was in the initial casting of *A Midsummer Night's Dream.* It soon became obvious how complicated it was going to be, as everyone wanted to appear in the play. But within a co-op, individuals are needed to undertake administrative roles, which are just as important as the acting roles, but less coveted. The round-table model did not work well. He recognized that a hierarchical business model was needed, but this view was not shared by some of the others in the group. Christopher described this period as "when all hell breaks loose." With the benefit of hindsight, he described the tension in his 2004 Artistic Director's Report to the Bard on the Beach Board:

It had been a difficult time as we struggled to find a way forward following the first season. There had been differing views on the kind of company we should become. I was sure that price, location, accessibility, and the open-backed tent were all vital components to our foundation. But I desired a company that was traditionally operated by an Artistic Director and General Manager, and I was firmly opposed to the view of a co-operative management. I was supported in this ideology by five community Board members, and we separated from the original group and incorporated the project "Bard on the Beach" into a theatre society. Now we had a shared direction, a plan, a defined project that had shown great potential. The rest, as they say, is history. But those early days were not easy. Creating theatre companies is hard and requires commitment, sacrifice, and an overwhelming desire to accomplish the task.

As I gained insight into this division and an understanding of the personal commitment Christopher Gaze had in ensuring the success of the Company, the words of one designer I interviewed seemed revealing: "I was asked to do the show the next year (1991), and there was a rift in the Company, as you probably know. The reason I stayed is that Christopher actually contacted me personally. The others sent out an impersonal contact, so

I thought I would talk to the person who actually speaks to me. Christopher chose to talk and he wanted me to return."

During these turbulent times, the assets, such as they were, had to be distributed between the two factions. They amounted to some costumes, about $6,000, and the name Bard on the Beach. At the time, Christopher wanted the funds and was prepared to let the name go, but Bard's publicist, Maureen Verkaar, present at one of the meetings, persuaded him that the name was worth more than the $6,000. When the group split, Christopher and his Board incorporated the name Bard on the Beach Theatre Society and "let Full House have the $6,000." During my interviews, various members of the Bard community reflected on this initial rocky start and the relationships that suffered as a result, a consequence that took a while to heal but now seems to be well forgotten (with some of the original actors subsequently appearing in and directing Bard productions).

So in early 1991, Bard on the Beach had the name but no money and had to start again. Fundraising began in earnest for the following season. It was decided they would offer two plays, *A Midsummer Night's Dream* and *As You Like It*. Christopher describes *Dream* as being programmatically "the magic play" but did not want the same adaptation as in 1990. He approached Scott Swan, who had directed the successful production in Edmonton in 1980, and persuaded him to do it in Vancouver. It was a huge success.

Almost eleven thousand people saw the forty-seven performances of *As You Like It* and *A Midsummer Night's Dream* the following year (1991), sitting on (very) hard wooden seats borrowed from the Vancouver School Board. The Company still operated by everyone pitching in and undertaking the tasks necessary to create the funding and logistics needed for the performances and for the Company to survive, with actors tasked to work during the intermission selling at the concession, in costume. Early patrons have recounted stories of Christopher dressed in Elizabethan robes and wearing heavy stage makeup wandering the Village chattering to patrons during the intermission, a legacy that remains today (without the costume). A number of these initial activities were described to me during interviews to illustrate how Bard managed to keep its head above water in the early days:

ONE Individuals packaging bags of candies in a volunteer's home in order to sell them during the intermission. Originally, candies of "questionable nutritional value" were sold, but this practice was discouraged as the Company grew, as Sarah Gaze explained. "The first year we had odd things like red licorice, but then we were pulled into the direction of the Birkenstock and we had to go slightly healthier because that was the clientele at the time."

TWO Christopher's aunt, in England, made pressed-flower cards and these were shipped out to Vancouver "at our and her expense," recalled Sarah. "And they sold very well. Basically, the concession had no items to sell other than the flower cards, cake, and candies."

THREE Board members helped with the stamping of tickets in one of their homes.

FOUR "Pie and Pint Nights" took place at the Town Pump and then the Unicorn Pub in Vancouver. These occurred during the winter months to keep the Bard name alive. Board members would sell tickets at twenty dollars each to whomever they knew, and for this sum, patrons received a pint of Shaftebury ale, a salad, and a pie of their choice.

FIVE Casino nights. Sarah Gaze recalled these well: "Oh my gosh, we used to go and do those terrible nights at the casino, a hell hole at Fraser and Marine near the Superstore. So that was a three o'clock-in-the-morning thing, but we got a lot of money; in those days we did it every year, and we did very well, if you got the right night, Friday or Saturday, which is what you wanted."

SIX Raffle tickets were sold at each performance, with the big prize in 1991 being a trip for two to England, from Cathay Pacific.

The 1991 Annual Report describes Christopher Gaze as being "The Heart and Soul of Bard on the Beach." As President Grant Burnyeat, who served from 1990 to 1991, wrote:

> It is hard to think of this as being the first AGM of the Bard on the Beach Theatre Society. In less than a year, we have accomplished so much—put together a Board of dedicated volunteers, raised enough money to finance our two theatre productions, obtained charitable status so we can now issue our own tax receipts, and arranged for the many volunteers that make our two productions possible. We have in excess of one hundred volunteers, one hundred members . . . All the founding members are committed to establishing a permanent Shakespeare season to rival Ashland, Oregon and Stratford.

In 1991, Bard made a $7,000 profit. The actors were paid $2,000 out of the co-op. The AGM of the Bard on the Beach Theatre Society was held on December 1 at The Town Pump pub in Vancouver and lasted thirty-five minutes. The minutes of that meeting do not fill a page.

The Early Years: 1992–1994
(The Lover)

"Though this be madness, yet there is method in 't." HAMLET

In one interview with Christopher, I asked if there was ever a time when he did not have fun at Bard. The year that sprang to his mind was 1992. During that season, one of the actors who'd been hired resented some of his fundraising techniques, particularly when Christopher "sold" a portion of this actor's part to someone for $220. The actor apparently "hit the roof" and got his colleagues involved. "A lot of the Company hated me; they booed me and all kinds of things," recalled Christopher. "I remember Scott Bellis, God bless him, saved the day. He said, 'I've got two parts, why doesn't the person come onto the stage and take my part.' I have always been grateful to Scott for that. That summer of 1992, this actor fractionalized the Company, and I remember feeling very, very lonely that summer, and unhappy. It was a long summer."

Christopher went on to explain that it is more important to have a cohesive company whose positive energy floods across into the audience than an extraordinary actor who creates trouble backstage, making everyone unhappy. Interestingly,

one of the current Bard management team also stressed the importance of a collegial atmosphere among actors, particularly with such a long performance season (see Act IV). So it would appear being an outstanding actor is not the only attribute that Bard cast members need. Christopher's experience in 1992 had a lasting influence—actors are considered not only for their onstage abilities but also for their ability to "fit into" the Bard family, as this group spends five months together.

The year 1992 also produced challenges in other ways. A new tent was purchased with the assistance of Communication Canada and the Vancouver Foundation, enabling audiences to grow to 520 per night. This tent was used until 2010. In 1992, 22,300 people attended sixty performances of *Twelfth Night* and *The Tempest*, doubling the audience size from the previous year. Revenue increased to over $306,000. Average attendance was an impressive 84 percent, with thirty-four of the sixty performances sold out. The cast consisted of twenty-one actors. Some of the actors, designers, and technicians had been with the Company since 1990.

TOP ❯ *Colin Heath and Christoper Gaze in* Twelfth Night, *1992.*

BOTTOM ❯ Twelfth Night, *1992.*

The budget allowed Bard to employ thirteen professional actors, a production stage manager, two directors, and a choreographer. They also employed eight non-professional actors and over twenty-five additional staff.

As Christopher wrote in his 1992 Annual Report to the Board, the excellent box-office receipts that season enabled Bard to pay the artists a bonus of $574 each. And for the first time, Christopher became an employee of the Company, as Artistic Director/General Manager, albeit on a minimal salary.

Even in those early days, Bard was able to offer young actors and technicians work experience with seasoned professionals and a stable four-month contract, increasing their knowledge of every aspect of theatre and giving tremendous exposure to potential employees. Bard had created one of the very few vehicles in Western Canada for actors to gain exposure to the classics, a legacy that remains today.

Two highly acclaimed directors, Scott Swan and Christopher's long-time friend and mentor, Douglas Campbell, directed the 1992 performances, adding to the quality of the productions. "Douglas Campbell was a huge boon to the Company when he came in 1992," recalled one designer, "as he brought a world vision to theatre. He came for many seasons and, in a sense, it revived his own life in the theatre—he felt respected and honoured—and in 1997 he went back to Stratford and directed a superb production of *Oedipus* with his son

ABOVE ⌃ *Torquil Campbell and Christine Guidies* in Romeo and Juliet, *1993*

OPPOSITE TOP ‹ The Tempest, *1992.*

OPPOSITE BOTTOM ‹ *Ashley Wright, Dean Paul Gibson, and Scott Bellis in* The Taming of the Shrew, *1993.*

Ben in the title role. He encouraged other directors from Stratford to work with us, and it began to give us a national profile and unique and important influences. This infusion of excitement into our work is what helps to make Bard special."

Although there was growth and success, money was still very tight. There was no room for extravagances. Sarah Gaze recalled an accountant Bard hired very early on. "Once the budget, which was very small, had been decided, that was it, you couldn't go to her and say, 'Can we have a wig for so and so?' She'd say no because [we] have not got the money for it. She was strict, so strict, but that is what we had to have. We could not have done it without these people who were so, so tight with the money. She was fabulous."

Despite a tight control on finances, Christopher shared in the 1992 Annual Report his hopes that remuneration for actors be increased:

I have recently concluded negotiations with Equity concerning 1993, and we are now in a position to offer performers $375.00 per week. Though still a concession rate, it represents a 46% increase over 1992 rates. Provided the Canada Council, the City and the province support our efforts, and our Board of Directors meets its fundraising goal, we should be able to pay actors the Canadian Theatre Agreement scale fees the following year . . . Our 1993 budget of $357,000.00 includes

$246,000.00 in salaries. This is the "measure of our respect" for our artists and employees.

Andrew Seal took over as President of the Board from Grant Burnyeat for a two-year period (1992 and 1993), whereupon his demands as Associate Dean of Medicine at UBC meant he found it necessary to step down; he was then replaced by Ken Affleck, who remained President until 2008. In 1993, box-office revenue was over $280,000, with a total income of over $500,000 (expenses were $470,000). There was no grant from Canada Council for the Arts, despite yearly applications; indeed, the entire income from grants was only $23,460, whereas money from donations was $24,117. The casino night earned the Company over $40,000, the concession over $32,000, and the raffle over $15,000. This year (1993) saw the scheduling of *The Taming of the Shrew* as well as Bard's first tragedy, *Romeo and Juliet*. Christopher felt his audience was maturing and would welcome seeing a play with greater challenges. This was also the year the Company began offering a number of lectures in conjunction with performances to further entertain and educate its patrons, a legacy that remains today.

As the years passed, fundraising activities became more ambitious. In February 1993, Bard rented the ballroom of the Fairmont Hotel and had a silent auction, a live auction, and a raffle for two nights at the Ritz Hotel in London. Sarah Gaze recalled

▲ King Lear, *1994*.

▲ *Douglas Campbell in* King Lear, *1994.*

the "extraordinary generosity" of people who donated to the auction. "I suppose they were the people who could see there was something here that was going to grow."

In 1994, box-office revenue had increased to $416,496, with ticket prices at $15, while total income was almost $700,000. Expenses were $681,888, so there was little wiggle room. Despite this, then President of the Board Ken Affleck wrote in the Annual Report, "There can be few Presidents of theatre societies in Canada, or perhaps anywhere, who find the task of reporting at their AGM as enjoyable as I do. Bard on the Beach has a record of unrivalled success. Perhaps our biggest problem is to maintain sufficient humility and avoid envious stares."

Despite these giddy growth times, Christopher Gaze recalled cash flow being an endless crisis "because we didn't have any." In his twenty-five-year recollection, *Gazing Back*, he describes how, as late as 1996, Board members would regularly allocate five to six thousand dollars from their own credit cards to Bard to ensure there was enough funding at the start of the season, with no firm guarantee they would get it back at the end of August. But they did. He also recalled walking to the bank late at night with an evening's takings, ever aware that anyone could be watching to steal them.

There was, however, a price to pay for Bard's early success and Christopher's commitment to it. In 1994, his fourteen-year marriage failed. He recalled how, in the early years of Bard, his home life changed as he became deeply immersed and involved in developing the Company. "I had been a very hands-on father to my sons, but my work took over, and so the dynamic of my marriage shifted. I never believed I would leave my marriage, but in the fall of 1994, I knew I could not go on, and I left the family home. It was a dreadful time and took years to recover from—for all of us—but recover we did. Life went on, I worked and worked and worked. I provided for my family, and as Bard bloomed, so did my lads. My sons are now men, and I am wonderfully close with them, their wives, and our beautiful grand-children. The Bard adventure has been a magnificent journey, but there have been sacrifices that have brought both great happiness and great sadness . . . I know no other way to explain it but that 'the web of our life is of a mingled yarn, good and ill together.'"

After reading the Annual Reports and speaking to many who were connected to Bard's early years, I am struck by the considerable commitment and energy that those involved in the early days had for the concept, which was no doubt buoyed by rapid growth. The Company did not waver from conveying the four-pronged message of delivering *Shakespeare,* at a unique *venue,* in an *affordable* and *accessible* manner to Vancouverites, tapping into an obvious demand. Twenty-eight years later, when audience members arrive at the very professional Bard Village, few appreciate just how difficult and challenging those early days were.

The Growth Years: 1995–2005
(The Soldier)

"Such stuff as dreams are made on."
THE TEMPEST

The AGM reports during this ten-year period, without exception, dis-cuss climate. Weather—specifically bad, wet weather and cold temperatures—was mentioned by almost every individual I interviewed for this study. It has been a subject of constant discussion over Bard's entire existence because it has such a dir-ect, unpredictable effect on this theatre group. Frequently, seasons start with rain and cold temperatures 'and genu-ine concern that attendance will not meet financial projections, but once the summer starts and temperatures soar, revenues increase and projections are achieved.

In 1995, weather was not the only chal-lenge for Bard. Christopher recounted a discussion at the Bard Board table about whether to increase ticket prices by a dollar. "It was decided that affordability was key and therefore we should keep the same price as the previous year. At the end of the season, we regretted this deci-sion as we lost $33,000 . . . I seem to recall we had an audience of 33,000, so if we'd increased the ticket price by a dollar, we

LEFT ◂ A Midsummer Night's Dream, *Bard in the Vineyard, 2003.*

BOTTOM ▾ *Jennifer Lines and Christopher Gaze in* The Merchant of Venice, *1996.*

would have broken even! Heigh-ho, the best laid plans . . ."

That same year, Bard performed on top of Grouse Mountain (about a twenty-minute drive from downtown Vancouver to the base of the mountain, whereupon a gondola is taken to the summit). Reflecting on the challenges encountered in offering this exciting venue for Shakespeare, Christopher recalled Saturday afternoon performances on Grouse, then dashing back down to do a performance at Bard in the evening. "I thought it would add a little panache to our brand, as well as some extra dollars to our box-office revenue—and it did. We did this for several years until it rained one year and we forfeited our fee." It was a bad blow at the time, but it led them to begin doing matinees at Bard on Saturdays, which created new revenue. "As I look back, I recognize that it was all part of the evolution of Bard—we made mistakes, but at least we were bold and innovative."

In 1998, Bard played another off-site venue—Christ Church Cathedral in Vancouver. Christopher was close friends with "two great men" of the Church, Dean Peter Elliott and Archbishop David Somerville, who agreed it would be a good idea to do an alfresco performance at the Cathedral. "And it was a good idea—the law company Lawson Lundell sponsored it, and we sold out. So it was great financially, but we felt it was a compromised experience. Once again, we were reminded that the best place to do our shows was at Bard."

Through this experience Christopher became acquainted and then friends with Anthony von Mandl, who he describes as a "brilliant visionary." Anthony was creating an extraordinary winery in the Okanagan at Mission Hill, situated across from Kelowna, overlooking Lake Okanagan, about a five-hour drive from Vancouver. They talked of creating a Shakespeare production that would play at the beautiful amphitheatre Anthony was building and came up with the project name Bard in the Vineyard. Christopher directed a production of *A Midsummer Night's Dream,* and they scheduled a run of twenty-eight performances. The production was wonderfully received, and thousands of people flocked to see the show. "It was all so elegant, accessible, and fun," recalled Christopher. "You could dine on the terrace prior to the show, or have canapés and glasses of wine on the grass and admire the architecture and ambiance of this most magnificent of wineries. Then the audience sat in the tiered amphitheatre and watched the show, the exquisite sunset, and the stars twinkling above—pure magic." Then in mid-August, a massive forest fire swept toward Kelowna on the other side of the lake, burning many homes and causing great hardship. "Ash fell from the sky, and smoke was heavy in the air. From Mission Hill, you could see houses in Kelowna go up in flames like Roman candles—it was terrible." Surprisingly, Bard lost only two performances and then another later on when the rain came. When all was said and done, eleven thousand people attended and they broke even on the venture.

Still, after that season finished, the Okanagan venture was deemed something Bard did not wish to continue. It had been very hard on the management team being so far away from their home venue, and the logistics were extremely complicated. Also, a great icon of Vancouver theatre, John Juliani, died while his son Alessandro was playing Lysander in this Bard in the Vineyard run. In retrospect, Christopher regretted the decision not to continue and looks forward to a time when Bard can return to the Okanagan. "We can see huge potential . . . for ourselves, for British Columbia, and for the community that resides there."

Despite these challenges, in true Christopher Gaze style, he maintained that the Company should not stop pioneering. And it did not. The period from 1995 to 2005 saw a number of initiatives introduced, grown, and expanded. Not only did the numbers attending performances climb, but the Company also invested in infrastructure. In 1995, padded seats were introduced after removal

of the old wooden seating. With many performances being over three hours in length, this was a very welcome change (as I know from first-hand experience). Probably the most significant structural change during this period was the introduction of the Studio Stage, which marked Bard's tenth anniversary in 1999. Named after Christopher's mentor, the Douglas Campbell Studio Stage opened despite acknowledgement that it would create challenges, not least of which was the acquisition of a new audience. These fears proved to be totally unfounded. In 1999, the Mainstage played to 96 percent capacity while the Studio, which showed just one play, *Measure For Measure*, was at 100 percent, a figure maintained for the following three years. In 2005, the Studio Stage expanded to include two productions. While this meant increased production costs, "It was an enormous success," recalled Christopher. "We sold every ticket . . . remarkably, both shows sold out weeks before the end of their runs."

Over this decade, not only was the number of plays increased, from two to four, but the length of the season also grew. While so many theatre companies experience issues attracting audiences and playing to half-empty houses, Bard's capacity never dropped below 90 percent. How many theatre companies can boast this?

In 2002, the gift shop was rebuilt, and the box office grew to accommodate more staff. Information kiosks were added to the Village in 2004, which resulted in an additional hundred new members signing up. Also in 2004, Bard's long-standing scenic designer, Pam Johnson, was asked to update the physical setting of the Bard Village, providing a larger entrance way, better lighting, easier and more welcoming traffic flow, and more space for sponsor recognition. The updates were inspired by one of Bard's technical staff, who commented that the Village had a somewhat dated "Ye Olde British" theme with dark wooden timber. "I said, 'We are in a park, so it should feel like a garden party,'" recalled Pam Johnson. "So we went yellow and white, picket fencing to delineate space, white fencing, and a light entranceway. We wanted something dramatic and grand."

Along the way, relationships with other arts organizations—particularly the VSO and Chor Leoni Men's Choir—continued to flourish, while the ever-popular fireworks nights drew significant numbers and enhanced box-office revenues. And while the workload and responsibilities seemed to "have no end," Christopher took great satisfaction in the sold-out performances night after night and "witnessing the delight and pleasure of our audiences. Without question, we run against the flow of what is experienced by other theatre companies and arts organizations in this country."

The period from 1995 to 2005 also saw some production milestones. Bard consulted with the Canadian Jewish Congress in order to produce *The Merchant of Venice* in Vancouver for the first time in over twenty years. *Cymbeline*, a Shakespearean play many have not heard of, was performed in 2002 and managed to achieve critical acclaim, and in 2004, Douglas Campbell, aged 82, played in *Macbeth* in the theatre that bore his name. Prior to this, in 1994, Campbell played as King Lear through one of the hottest Augusts on record, prompting Board President Ken Affleck to be "perpetually worried we would need to find a new King Lear before the season was over. Douglas Campbell was brilliant and survived."

Throughout this period, audiences grew and Bard began gaining international recognition. In 2003, Christopher's good friend Maestro Bramwell Tovey called with huge excitement from Europe after he read an article by Patrick Carnegy in the UK's prestigious *Spectator* magazine, excerpted here:

> *Transported to Seattle as a speaker in a symposium to help launch that Wagner mecca's new* Parsifal, *I had the good fortune, a day or so later, to find myself beached up, quite literally, on the Pacific shoreline at Vanier Park in Vancouver. There, in the tented village of Bard on the Beach, I happened upon a delightfully accomplished Pericles (given as though performed by Victorian strolling players, adept in the mask techniques and stylised movement of commedia dell'arte). This play, together with* The Comedy of Errors *and* The Merchant, *makes up this summer's 'B on the B' festival,*

the most enterprising venture of its kind in Western Canada. Founded in 1990 by Christopher Gaze, graduate of the Bristol Old Vic, and still run by him, the three-month festival is now playing to around 70,000 and thriving without public subsidy. It's doing so well that Gaze has just inaugurated Bard in the Vineyard by directing A Midsummer Night's Dream *in a 600-seater amphitheatre in the heart of British Columbia's wineries, some four hours' drive east from Vancouver. If the Royal Shakespeare Company should need a temporary home while rebuilding at Stratford, it could do worse than look at Bard on the Beach's two beautifully designed tents. Erected on the meadows by the Avon, they would lack only B on the B's breathtaking ability to open up the rear canvas and play against a backdrop of English Bay with the mountains rising up behind. Imagine what this was able to do for the comings and goings of gondolas in* The Merchant. *Maybe a little of that could also be managed on the Avon?*

PAGES 66–67 ‹ *Chor Leoni, 2015.*

TOP LEFT ‹ *Douglas Campbell in* Macbeth, *2004.*

TOP RIGHT ‹ *Don Adams in* Macbeth, *2004.*

BOTTOM ‹ *Much Ado About Nothing, 2004.*

And while all these activities and accolades were taking place, the educational component of Bard continued to flourish behind the scenes. An increasing number of young people took part in the Bard workshops, which operated to capacity in the summer months. As Christopher explained, "The collective fallout of these activities that we offer does so much for education, for life skills, and for building a richer sense of self and culture in the minds of children. We have become an important educational resource for BC, and our existence plays a vital role in our society." These workshops, originally initiated in 1995 by Moira Wylie, the wife of Douglas Campbell, grew through this decade to become an established aspect of Bard (see Act V).

Despite unsuccessful yearly applications for Canada Council for the Arts grants, Bard continued to grow and thrive. Although busy, Christopher also found time to fall in love. He met Jennifer in late 2000, and they were married two years later. Jennifer Gaze recalled meeting for their "first real date" at the Orpheum. "I was nervous and he was nervous—I could tell. We went in and he said, 'Would you like the ladies' [room], would you like a cup of tea?' and I thought, no guy has ever asked me if I would like the ladies' [room] before I go into a show. He thinks about other people. He is the consummate gentleman."

When asked about her courtship with such a busy man, she recalled attending a lot of performances, but always making time for each other, a trait that continues as they both negotiate full lives. Whenever Christopher is thanking those who support Bard, he never fails to acknowledge his spouse, and many of my interviewees also commented on the devotion evident in their partnership. Christopher recalled "the true turning point" of meeting Jennifer in December 2000. "We fell in love at first sight and married with great fanfare at Christ Church Cathedral on December 1, 2002. Over the years, Jennifer has become the "Green Queen" at Bard, and as our love and life together blossomed, so did the greenness of Bard! Every evening when I go to welcome our audiences at Bard and introduce the shows, Jennifer invariably comes, too, and chats to the theatre patrons, volunteers and staff. We are a double act, and I cannot imagine doing what I do at Bard, or with our family, without the incandescent presence of her."

⌃ *Moya O'Connell and Bob Frazer in* Hamlet, *2005.*

The Establishment Years: 2005–2010 *(The Judge)*

"True is it that we have seen better days." AS YOU LIKE IT

The year 2005 was a banner one for Bard, with record attendance, four critically acclaimed productions, and growing individual and corporate support. And for the next five years, this scenario continued. Bard was going from strength to strength, and if there were any storm clouds gathering on the horizon, they were being ignored. Numbers continued to grow as more and more Vancouverites and visitors came to enjoy Bard's unique offering—"a complete experience," as one former employee commented. After sixteen years, Bard was presenting four high-class productions each year and offering something different. While theatregoers may have attended other productions because of the show on offer, many were attending Bard because it had become a highly enjoyable annual tradition. As described by one member of Bard management, "It's the experience you get when you come to the site for the first time. Coming out at intermission and watching the sunset, it creates a special feeling for people . . . And so that is what makes it different."

ABOVE ⏶ *Bob Frazer, Stephen Holmes, and Haig Sutherland in* Rosencrantz and Guildenstern Are Dead, *2005.*

RIGHT ⏵ *Haig Sutherland and Stephen Holmes in* Rosencrantz and Guildenstern Are Dead, *2005.*

OPPOSITE TOP LEFT ‹ *Josue Laboucane, Tara Jean Wilkin, and Parnelli Parnes in* A Midsummer Night's Dream, *2006.*

OPPOSITE TOP RIGHT ‹ *Tara Jean Wilkin, Parnelli Parnes, Josue Laboucane, and Melissa Poll in* A Midsummer Night's Dream, *2006.*

OPPOSITE BOTTOM ‹ *Scott Bellis and Colleen Wheeler in* A Midsummer Night's Dream, *2006.*

RIGHT › *Bob Frazer and Colleen Wheeler in* The Taming of the Shrew, *2007.*

Bard also staged its second non-Shakespeare play in 2005 (the first was in 1996 when *Shylock* by Mark Leiren-Young was performed). Tom Stoppard's *Rosencrantz and Guildenstern Are Dead* sold out weeks before the end of its run. During the following years, performances continued to sell out. In 2008, *Twelfth Night* broke the $1 million mark in box-office revenue, with over 87,000 people attending the four performances that year. There were, however, devastating events, most notably the death of Douglas Campbell in 2009, whose influence on Christopher Gaze and Bard had been paramount. Despite the personal tragedies, the artistic strength of the Company continued to flourish during this period. In 2009, Christopher Gaze wrote in the Annual Report that the quality of Bard rivalled anything in Canada, and maybe internationally. The annual reports for the period were perpetually optimistic, as it seemed Bard could do no wrong.

OPPOSITE TOP ‹ *Jennifer Lines and Colleen Wheeler in* The Comedy of Errors, *2009.*

OPPOSITE BOTTOM ‹ *Alessandro Juliani in* Henry V, *2010.*

RIGHT › *Charlie Gallant and David Marr in* Falstaff, *2010.*

BOTTOM ⌄ *Tiffany Lyndall-Knight, Christopher Gaze, and Lois Anderson in* King Lear, *2008.*

While this giddy growth was occurring, attention was focused on the artistic quality of the performances but not on the supporting infrastructure. Ironically, it was often during the off-season (October to April) that staff felt the most challenged. Bard recruited part-time staff for the summer season and had a bank of volunteers to draw upon, but in the non-performance months, staffing levels were reduced to a slim core. Actors had the Canadian Theatre Agreement (CTA) to ensure that their personal and professional well-being was being addressed. The "behind the scenes" administration did not. Bard had been rapidly growing without the necessary growth in the supporting administration. It was a crisis waiting to happen.

And in 2010 a crisis occurred. As outlined in the Managing Director's Report that year, as the final lights were being hung in the Mainstage tent, a member of the technical team noticed a deformed portion of the tent's truss. After the engineer inspected it, it was determined that a section of pipe needed to be replaced. Unfortunately, the only way to replace it was to lay the tent down, after first removing the lights, speakers, seats, sets, and portions of the risers and stage. Performances would have to be cancelled only five days before the first scheduled show.

The fix itself took only one day to complete. However, clearing the tent, laying it down, re-erecting it, and resetting the audience and stage areas took an additional five days. Nine performances were cancelled, with over 1,500 student tickets cancelled outright and another 2,500 regular tickets rebooked or refunded. Over 4,600 tickets were pulled out of inventory, representing potential lost ticket and retail revenue of about $117,000. Additional staff, engineering, crane time, rentals, materials, and other related costs pushed the financial impact over $150,000.

Although financial reserves did exist to cope with this, it placed huge stress on the small number of personnel. The core administrative team had to take on numerous additional tasks to handle whatever was required. The impact on the box office was particularly significant, as a massive rescheduling task was required. At this point, a number of long-term staff left. Christopher Gaze described it as a "landmark year for Bard."

As Board Chair John McCulloch, who had taken over as chair in 2008, noted in the 2011 Annual Report, "The President's report this year is far more subdued than we have perhaps become used to, as for the first time in several years we cannot report success and growth in the way we have become accustomed."

With the benefit of hindsight, it is easy to understand what occurred. Bard had invested heavily in its performances and in delivering quality work to its ever-growing, appreciative audiences, but had ignored the Company's management and administrative infrastructure needs. The management team's commitment to the Bard family, working long hours and performing any task assigned, was sustainable while the Company was small. As Bard continued to grow, it was not.

[SCENE VI]

The Turbulent Years:
2011–2013 *(The Old Man)*

"When sorrows come, they come
not single spies, but in battalions."
HAMLET

⌃ *Kayvon Khoshkam and John Murphy in* The
Merchant of Venice, *2011.*

The introduction of reserved seating in 2011 meant that patrons no longer had to rush into the theatre and place blankets/coats/bags/sweaters on a seat to secure it. Pre-assigned seats had been discussed for a number of years before they were finally introduced. Bard had even supplied sticky notes for patrons to secure their seat. General admission seating had been one of those iconic characteristics of Bard—adored by some, hated by others—so reserved seating was a huge structural change. As a member of Bard management explained, "It was about how people thought about coming to Bard; they thought about lining up, and people would wait for two to three hours. They would be in line and it would be a social time, then they would run in with their stickies and put them on their chairs, so it just became this heightened thing, and it created a lot of demand, but it restricted us in a lot of ways."

A Board member recalled people lining up at 5 PM for an 8 PM show. "There were whole rituals—people would do different things; people had picnics. This sort

of family atmosphere in the line, which we used to have, doesn't exist anymore. Don't get me wrong, nine out of ten people were ecstatic we went to reserve seating, and there were a lot of people who really disliked having to wait in line. And we got complaints the first year and a couple in the second year, but we don't get any complaints about it anymore. People have adjusted and they realize how much nicer it is to walk into a theatre and know where they are going to sit."

While reserved seating replaced one of the much-loved, long-standing, unique traditions at Bard, this change was not as dramatic as the introduction of the new 740-seat Mainstage tent. Fundraising for this new structure started in 2008, but was stepped up in 2010 when the old tent failed and it became obvious a new structure was rapidly required. Bard managed to raise $3.4 million in seven months from a concerted fundraising campaign led by Vancouver developer Bruno Wall and assisted by a well organized and committed group of Board members and supporters.

One Board member recalled his experience of the campaign: "Raising money is kind of funny; it's kind of uncomfortable, but whenever you do it, it makes you feel good. I had no background . . . so it was really just a system of going out and talking to people about the project. Bruno had a lot of contacts, I had contacts, the Board had contacts, Christopher had contacts—he knows everybody in the city, he is amazing—so it was a combination of all that."

OPPOSITE TOP ‹ *Todd Thomson and Robert Olguin in* Twelfth Night, *2013.*

OPPOSITE BOTTOM ‹ *Todd Thomson and Rachel Cairns in* Twelfth Night, *2013.*

ABOVE ⌃ *Richard Newman in* The Merchant of Venice, *2011.*

OPPOSITE ‹ *Patti Allan in* The Merry Wives of Windsor, *2012.*

ABOVE LEFT ˄ *Lois Anderson in* Measure For Measure, *2013.*

ABOVE RIGHT ˄ *Kevin Kruchkywich in* The Taming of the Shrew, *2012.*

Unlike the previous tents, which had been ordered "off the peg," this one was custom-made, designed with the help of Proscenium Architects, a firm in Vancouver. The steel structures were manufactured in the US, with the canvas obtained from a company in New Zealand. The house risers were from a firm in England, and the theatre seating shipped from Australia.

The introduction of the new tent was a watershed moment for Bard. The cost of the structure, together with its construction, the addition of a new stage, and the new seating system, amounted to significant challenges in 2011. Although most items were delivered on time, the installation was significantly slower than expected, resulting in considerable additional construction and labour costs. At the time, management did not know whether some of these expenditures would be permanent and ongoing or could be explained by the fact that it was the first time the operation had been undertaken and, with more experience, would be reduced. In 2011, Bard was in uncharted, turbulent waters.

While the tent was delivered on schedule, the risers and seating were not, which meant that staff and volunteers had to be trained without the final structure being in place. The new tent also produced challenges acoustically, as Christopher explained after the first season: "How does one play to an audience of 740 in a large tent and not yell, nor be overly operatic, yet emotionally reach and connect with the audience?" Although five thousand more people attended Bard in 2011, this number was not as high as hoped and clearly fell short of the numbers needed to fill the new structure. Upon reflection, a Board member suggested that insufficient thought had been given to the increased marketing required to attract additional patrons. To further compound all issues and add insult to injury, June was wet, miserable, and cold.

All told, 2011 was not a good year. Poor weather, weak attendance, poor acoustics, and a costly new structure that was unfamiliar meant that, for the first time in its history, Bard was experiencing some major challenges. With over twenty years of unbridled success, the organization was not acquainted with stumbling.

The issues encountered in 2011 were compounded the following year, as Bard failed to generate the income needed to sustain the higher infrastructure costs. In 2012, two long-time management staff, the managing director and the bookkeeper, left. In 2013, one of the struts on the Studio Stage collapsed, requiring a replacement tent one year earlier than planned. Cost overruns, and coping with a new venue, thrust the organization into financial crisis. With the long-time bookkeeper gone and capital and construction expenses increasing, it soon became obvious to the Board that the financial health of the organization was failing. Bard had been a "mom and pop" organization with wonderful, committed people who were willing to give up their time and give up themselves, but in 2012 the point had been reached when this was not enough.

For the first time, the Board had to accept that Bard had grown significantly and, to match and support this growth, a firmer management structure was required. As one member explained, "A lot of what we're talking about is good because it talks to the real. An organization doesn't just go from $2 to $6 million without challenges . . . I don't think there is anything to hide. It is an important part of the history."

Defined roles and job descriptions for staff were now needed. During these turbulent years, the Board took on a more active role. The President of the Board, John McCulloch, who had replaced Ken Affleck

▲ *Bob Frazer in* Macbeth, *2012.*

in 2008, took over as interim Managing Director. With John McCulloch now directing all his energies to the day-to-day running of Bard, Board member Jim Bovard took over as President. All this took place with the full support of Christopher who, with characteristic optimism, speculated that the three of them would act in unison, like the Three Musketeers, to address and solve Bard's issues.

For years and years, Bard had solid box-office revenues and of significant reserves, but new capital investment in infrastructure had depleted these. The expanded site, tent, and construction had increased the cost base permanently and needed to be budgeted for annually. While the Company was happy to spend on and invest in high-quality productions, it now needed to acknowledge that the larger tent and related costs required increased financing, and these costs would be ongoing.

One of the more experienced actors confessed that while he had little knowledge of what was going on financially within the organization, "Just by watching Christopher and how stressed out he appeared, that suggested there were a few seasons where things were touch and go." Those who knew him well were privy to these acute stresses, but as one Board member stated, "Even when we were having financial issues and recording was not as it could have been, or as we wanted it to be, Christopher was always upbeat—'Don't worry, we'll fix it; don't worry, it'll be great!'"

One of the few bright points in this challenging time was when the Vancouver International Wine Festival chose Bard as its beneficiary. It had previously raised funds for the Vancouver Playhouse, but when that theatre company folded, the Wine Festival undertook a process to find a replacement and selected Bard. It was, as one Board member described, "a very happy time for us."

In January 2014, after a period of negotiation, Claire Sakaki was appointed to take over as Executive Director. With an excellent track record, having worked in Toronto at the Soulpepper Theatre Company for fourteen years, Claire had been courted for a number of months by Board members and Christopher, and all were delighted with her decision. This enabled John McCulloch, the interim Managing Director, to step down. Described by one member of the Bard management team as a "Renaissance man," McCulloch had stepped in to undertake the unsexy work of reforming the structure of the organization, radically changing job descriptions and responsibilities, and revamping the financial systems. In McCulloch's words, "I learned a huge amount, not least that the theatre is a mad business of continual adrenalin rushes, highs and lows, crisis and emotion, amazing people, and precarious deadlines. I kid you not, it is not for anyone out there who has a 'normal' business life. It is not for the faint of heart."

> *Colleen Wheeler in* Elizabeth Rex, *2013.*

LEFT ‹ *Haig Sutherland in* Elizabeth Rex, *2013.*

RIGHT ▲ *Colleen Wheeler and Haig Sutherland in* Elizabeth Rex, *2013.*

OPPOSITE › *Jonathon Young and Jennifer Lines in* Hamlet, *2013.*

▲ *Allan Morgan in* The Tempest, *2014.*

The Recent Past and Future: 2014 Onward

(The Corpse—but Bard is a long way from dead)

"Life's uncertain voyage . . ."
TIMON OF ATHENS

Bard's twenty-fifth year was the most successful year in its history, playing to 93 percent capacity, with earned revenue up by 28 percent. "In 2014, it was madness and we went for broke," recalled one member of the management team. "We had *Midsummer*, we had *The Tempest*, and it was so vibrant. We had about 100,000 people. It was our twenty-fifth anniversary, and we just worked as hard as we could. Best ticket sales we ever did. Record attendance, the weather was wonderful, and it just clicked—it was fantastic. For the twenty-fifth anniversary, we got a lot of partnership and events—we had the Symphony for the first year, we had an improv troupe do Shakespeare, we had all these special events going on."

In 2014, Bard regained its footing and returned to the state of affairs it was used to—performing excellent Shakespeare to packed houses on a stable financial foundation. Lessons had been learned: when performing theatre in a temporary structure,

▲ *Luisa Jojic, Todd Thomson, and Naomi Wright in*
The Tempest, *2014.*

▲ *Shawn Macdonald, Anousha Alamian, and Anton Lipovetsky in* Equivocation, *2014.*

things can go wrong; reserves need to be created and maintained to ensure unforeseen circumstances can be fully addressed. As one actor explained, "It's really like watching someone grow up. It is an infant, then a toddler; it stumbled and fell and learned to walk, then learned to run."

As I discovered during the course of research for this book, there was unbridled support and admiration not only for Christopher Gaze but also for Claire Sakaki. In numerous interviews with Board members and management, I could sense the palpable relief all felt when recalling Claire Sakaki's acceptance of the position of Executive Director of Bard on the Beach in January 2014. Many recognized how close the Company was to failing, as stated by a Board member: "We were a sinking ship. That should be remembered." While it was the efforts of the Board members and interim Managing Director that essentially managed to turn the Company around, there was still a strong need for an Executive Director who could "tweak" the changes and oversee the safe and secure financial and managerial future of the Company. Claire's recruitment into the Bard family as a highly competent Executive Director with a solid track record meant the Board (and Christopher) could relax, take less of a hands-on role, and watch the Company develop on a stable business and artistic footing. As another Board member described, "Bard has grown organically,

⌃ *Benjamin Elliott and Shawn Macdonald in* Cymbeline, *2014.*

OPPOSITE TOP ‹ *Luisa Jojic and Benjamin Elliott in* The Comedy of Errors, *2014.*

OPPOSITE BOTTOM, CENTRE ‹ *Dawn Petten in* The Comedy of Errors, *2014.*

ABOVE LEFT ⌃ *Lili Beaudoin in* The Comedy of Errors, *2014.*

ABOVE RIGHT ⌃ *Sereana Malani and Lindsey Angell in* The Comedy of Errors, *2014.*

▲ *Lindsey Angell and Benjamin Elliott in* The Comedy of Errors, *2014.*

has always grown organically, and what is changing now is that we are adding more structure to it. I think we are at a point in time when we can look back and take stock; we are examining where we've been and where we want to go."

In October 2015, Bard moved into new offices and performance space (see Act III) on West 1st Avenue, at the exact place the Vancouver Playhouse had had its production centre. "They made an arrangement with the developer, Bruno Wall, and the City to create a cultural amenity in what would be a new development under two condominium towers," explained Christopher. "Sadly, the theatre company [Playhouse] did not survive to realize its dream, but Bard and the Arts Club collaborated to share the magnificent production centre that sits a stone's throw from the Olympic Village."

Many acknowledged the challenges of operating a theatre company from a tem-

LEFT ‹ *Dawn Petten in* Love's Labour's Lost, *2015.*

ABOVE ⌃ *Scott Bellis and Benedict Campbell in* King Lear, *2015.*

porary summer home, while at the same time recognizing its almost romantic ambiance. "Up until 2013, the whole Bard office moved to the site in the summer —phone systems, computer systems, everything," explained a member of the management team. "And you lived in tents in the park. It was like being in the middle of this magic thing. Yes, it was cold and miserable in the spring, and then someone would saw through a power line or the data line or the phone line or whatever, and you'd have to deal with that." Mixed feelings were also captured in one designer's comment: "You never move forward without leaving stuff behind, and it's hard for a company that is as community-oriented as we are to move away from things that we had in the past."

With its new home on West 1st Avenue, Bard experienced a coming of age. The challenges of the past have been addressed, the management structure is strong, lessons have been learned. The nightmares of failing tent structures and poor weather can be costed into insurance policies. And while Bard may have been remiss not to identify and address its managerial and financial issues dur-

ing the Company's rapid growth through the decades from 1990 to 2010, when issues finally were faced, it was the Board that pulled together and worked to sustain the organization and keep it afloat—stepping up fundraising campaigns, revamping job descriptions of personnel, and refining financial accounting methods. The Board President took over the Managing Director role and the day-to-day running of the organization to ensure it did not fail. Despite the arts' reputation for being a highly risky business, Bard now has an extensive, qualified staff, hierarchical structures (see Appendices), and new offices. Bad weather, poor reviews, structural failures, donor fatigue, plus 101 unforeseen circumstances can affect revenues, but in 2017 the future looks bright. The challenges of the last few years, while highly stressful at the time, have led to a stronger organization. As one Board member articulated, "Bard has gotten richer artistically, culturally, and financially. It's gotten richer and more vibrant and more confident and more daring, and therefore more exciting."

As another explained, "We were standing on one foot, trying to make sure we did not fall down, and now we are firmly standing on two feet, looking up. We've had new Board members, we've had new management, we've had our biggest season ever, and we have a new theatre. The last two years have been good. There have been really big, big changes over the last few years. I think now we are a real

organization—'I'm a real boy now,' said Pinocchio!"

As this Act concludes, it is important to look back to Bard's roots. In 1990, there was a tense division between the actors who decided to join Christopher and the others who wanted to continue to exist as a co-op. Twenty-eight years later, one of the original actors who did not join Christopher recalled the sense of pride and ownership felt now about Bard's success and about being involved with the original group:

The Company was founded by actors and a couple of design and technical guys, who have gone on to have formidable careers. What is that Margaret Mead thing—never underestimate the power of the individual. I think all actors need to [know that] they don't have to wait for that play, or wait for someone to invite them—you can go and make your own workshop. Since Bard, I've founded two companies. That's what I like so much about the story of the Company. It's a testament to what people working in the arts can do. ▶

OPPOSITE ◄ *Jay Hindle and Lindsey Angell in* Love's Labour's Lost, *2015.*

ABOVE ▲ *Josh Epstein and Luisa Jojic in* Love's Labour's Lost, *2015.*

ACT III

"I like this place, and willingly
could waste my time in it."

AS YOU LIKE IT

The S E T

The Administration Office

"This castle hath a pleasant seat; the air nimbly and sweetly recommends itself unto our gentle senses."

MACBETH

On September 18, 2015, Bard moved from the rented office space it had occupied for three years on a large urban thoroughfare (I expect by the time these words appear in print, the building will have been demolished) to the brand-new office and performance space shared with the Arts Club Theatre Company and known as the BMO Theatre Centre. This move signified a huge, highly visible step for Bard and a coming of age. As one designer explained, "Suddenly, having this building cuts out a huge amount of stress and uncertainty that we had to deal with. We have a space, and it's secure and supports the work we do."

While the Bard spaces open to the public (essentially the Bard Village) are clean, pleasant, well maintained, and welcoming—the sort of environment patrons like to spend time in—I must admit I was a little taken aback by the working office space when I initially met with Christopher Gaze in his former office in July 2015 to discuss this book.

Christopher then provided an account of the various locations Bard has occupied over its existence:

Over the past twenty-eight years, Bard has had several administrative homes. The first was in the basement of my home, and then we managed to afford to move to Vancouver's East Side in 1993. We were able to keep everything in the building—our costumes, tents, and two tiny offices. A few years later, we moved in with Ballet BC to the old Real Estate Board building. We also managed to keep everything there too, but it was getting tight. I remember the landlord wanted us to vacate the building at a very inconvenient time for us because he wanted to develop the site. I went to his home in Shaughnessy [an affluent area of Vancouver] to beg him to let us stay awhile longer. I knocked and knocked on his door. He finally opened it, a little tiny bit. I beseeched him to let us stay and offered him some Bard chocolate bars, which he took and quickly closed the door! Anyway, my gambit worked—we stayed until our newly renovated offices were ready, and then off we went to Cambie Street, above the stage door of the Vancouver Playhouse. We stayed in those offices for about five years and then grew out of them as well. So we found new offices that we rented from the City of

OPPOSITE AND THIS PAGE ‹ › *Bard's new head-quarters at the BMO Theatre Centre.*

Christopher Gaze at opening of the BMO Theatre Centre in November 2015.

Vancouver. Meanwhile, we had storage for all our sets, props, and costumes on East Hastings, but when that location was going to be redeveloped, we moved our storage location to Richmond. We still use our Richmond facility to store our ever-growing site infrastructure, but at the BMO Theatre Centre we have a fabulous costume-storage facility. We've come a long way!

The new 48,000-square-foot space is shared between the Arts Club and Bard. As explained by a member of the management team, the facility was originally earmarked for the Vancouver Playhouse, but when they folded in 2012, the City took proposals. It was a sad event that proved fortuitous for Bard. "So it ended up being Bard and the Arts Club . . . Bard inherited a number of things from the Playhouse, so it's bittersweet."

The $21-million space has been funded by the developers—Wall Centre, which provided the shell of the building ($7 million); the City of Vancouver, which contributed $7 million; Canadian Heritage, who gave $2.5 million; and the Province of British Columbia, which granted $1 million. The remaining sum was raised by Bard and the Arts Club. The lease is for sixty years.

The contrast between Bard's brand new location on West 1st Avenue and their previous office space could not be more striking. The top floor of the building houses the Bard offices, including Christopher's office, with abundant natural light from the floor-to-ceiling windows. Gone are all remnants of his old office. His space now displays artistic, framed photographs of past Bard productions, a shelving unit with books and family photographs, and a couch, tastefully clad in black leather to match the furniture. This floor also houses the Bard costume shop and the Arts Club offices. The main floor is home to the 240-seat Goldcorp Stage, as well as four rehearsal spaces, dressing rooms, bar, and reception area. There is a shared lounge facility for actors and staff, as well as a huge separate storage facility for costumes.

The fact that two arts bodies are sharing the facility a stone's throw away from central Vancouver promotes interaction within the theatre community where actors and theatre professionals working on different productions can come together and network. This brand-new, well-located, professional space is a solid testament and accolade to Bard's arrival and acceptance as a permanent and growing entity on the Vancouver arts scene. The physical presence and its long-term benefits to Bard are only just coming to be realized. At the time of writing, there is still unpacking to be done, while Vancouver's appreciation of a new theatre so close to the downtown core is starting to emerge.

The Bard Village

"I like this place, and willingly could waste my time in it." AS YOU LIKE IT

There is something unmistakably unique and iconic about walking to the Bard Village. Most patrons have already seen the distinctive white-and-red tents from afar—clearly visible from the Burrard Inlet as one crosses the Burrard Street Bridge, they are a fixture from April to September each year. The Village, set in Vanier Park, a stone's throw from the centre of Vancouver and on the oceanfront, is ringed by a simple fence and covers approximately 100,000 square feet. The land is owned by the federal government and managed by the Vancouver Park Board, which each year grants the Bard organization authority to use it, for which they pay a permit fee.

An actor I spoke with described the "festival effect" of walking through the park to get to the Village. "It's almost a pilgrimage. There is this feeling you are leaving the world behind, and that sounds a bit too poetic, but you do have to take this little journey. You walk past the trees to get to this tent in the middle of nowhere, and just the act of doing that is special. And then [there's] the lovely courtyard they have. Usually in theatres, there's a little entrance area; it feels more like a

swimming pool lobby in most theatres. Bard has this large circular courtyard—it feels more like a circus. It's more sociable. It makes you open to new things before you even sit down to watch the play, so when you see a new production you don't dismiss it—it's like you're marinating your brain to experience something new and different."

A member of the management team added, "Theatre at its heart is simultaneously transient and permanent. It is not like a form, it happens in a moment and then that moment is gone, but the effects of that moment last forever, so I think there is something about doing it in a space that captures that paradox and dichotomy."

The Village contains a number of public and private areas and two large performance tents—the BMO Mainstage in the Mainstage Theatre tent and the Howard Family Stage in the Douglas Campbell Theatre. It takes Bard two full months to establish a presence in Vanier Park, but only two weeks to tear it down. A crew of up to thirty individuals works seven days a week from 9 AM to 5 PM to build the site. I was told it costs approximately $750,000 to establish and remove the infrastructure. Collectively known as the Bard Village, the central, covered public area contains a concession, box office, and boutique gift store. Shiny white wooden seating is positioned among potted plants and hanging baskets. String lights illuminate the central gathering area as the evening descends. Numerous porta-potties are

lined up, and during the intermission, volunteers guide patrons to the vacant facilities. Patrons who arrive by vehicle (75 percent) park in the facilities of the Museum of Vancouver, a short five-minute walk from the Village. There is additional parking on some adjacent land. Bard also has a safe storage area for bikes.

Bard purchased its first five-hundred-seat saddle span tent in 1992, and used it until the end of the 2010 season. As outlined in Act II, during the summer of 2010 there were considerable issues with the structure, resulting in the cancellation of a number of performances. So in 2010, Bard launched the Staging Our Future campaign to raise capital for a new Mainstage theatre. The new tent was ready for the 2011 season and its stage was named after the Bank of Montreal in recognition of its lead contribution to their fundraising campaign. This structure featured the signature open backdrop, which is the emblem of Bard. It included a redesigned stage with 742 comfortable seats.

The Douglas Campbell Theatre tent was added in 1999 in celebration of Bard's tenth anniversary. This smaller theatre seats 240 people with an adaptive layout and seating configuration. In 2013, the tent itself was replaced, with funding from the Staging Our Future campaign. In

‹ *The Bard on the Beach Village site at Vanier Park.*

2014, the performance space was named the Howard Family Stage in recognition of Darlene Howard (a Board member) and Paul Howard, local philanthropists and strong supporters of Bard's theatrical and educational components.

In addition to the covered spaces, there are a couple of open grassy areas with picnic tables for participants to enjoy. The Bard Village is open one hour before the performance starts, and patrons can bring their own food and have a picnic with friends to extend the evening's enjoyment. "You can have superb acting anywhere, you can go and have a picnic anywhere," offered one Board member, "but in Bard you can have it in one place. It's magical."

As mentioned, in addition to the Bard Village's public spaces, there are additional tented structures. The box office sells and distributes tickets and also houses the on-site administration. Like most offices, there are computers, desks, chairs, paper, noticeboards, and screens, but because everything is temporary, there are very few personal accoutrements.

During the course of this research, a broad section of respondents, including volunteers, donors, patrons, management, and Board members, all commented on the one thing about Bard they did not like: the on-site toilet facilities. As one Board member declared with considerable understatement, "It would be awfully nice to have proper toilets." Others insightfully suggested that they were a great "social leveller" that have apparently improved over the years. Unfortunately, these facilities are currently the only available option. Bard is cognizant that they are not their most attractive feature, but is making every attempt to make the best of this provision. "We have thirty portable toilets that are not gender specific, as well as four accessible portable toilets, for the public," explained a member of the management team. "Typically, you'd want a ratio of one toilet per fifty to seventy-five people. We are higher than average, and we have some of the cleanest portables you've ever seen!"

A number of structures, routines, and experiences distinguish a visit to the Bard Village from attendance at other theatres. Many of those I interviewed argued that Bard was not stuffy or elitist and therefore more welcoming, with some patrons arriving in designer dresses and dinner jackets and others in flip-flops and shorts. Other traditions include:

ONE Allowing drinks and food into the theatre itself. Most theatres allow bottled water but nothing else. Bard allows everything, so there is no rush to gulp down wine or beer to accommodate the performance. Popcorn, chocolate, and cookies can also be consumed.

TWO Bringing blankets into the theatre. As the evening tempera-

ture drops, these are much needed. Likewise, sometimes sunglasses are useful if the sun is setting and your seat is positioned to experience this sunset. Blankets and fleece jackets are sold in the Bard Boutique. Interestingly, as time has elapsed, there is less discussion about cold temperatures in the tents but more about the heat. Global warming and climate change create a double-edged sword, encouraging more patrons to Bard when the weather is good, but if temperatures soar, it is challenging for actors wearing chain mail or heavy Elizabethan velvet gowns.

THREE Arriving an hour before the show to have a picnic. The Bard Village is equipped with white tables and chairs and mown grass to sit on. Opportunities to meet friends for sushi and wine in the Bard Village before the performance abound and, with no restrictions on patrons bringing their own food, costs are reduced and choices extended. Catered picnic baskets can also be ordered, and food trucks periodically stop by.

FOUR The Bard Boutique sells books, jewellery, clothing, and other Shakespeare-related merchandise. Few other more traditional theatrical venues do this. Each year, new merchandise is added (for example, in 2015, images of the original costume designs were made available for purchase). The boutique is a significant revenue source for the Company.

FIVE Full cast biographies and photographs are displayed.

SIX Enthusiastic volunteers engage patrons in lively discussions to solicit funding, but never with a "hard-sell" attitude.

SEVEN There is a designated area to leave bikes.

EIGHT As many patrons attend while holidaying in Vancouver, a map of the world, with pins showing where patrons are from, is displayed.

NINE Free full-colour programs promote all summer performances along with Bard's additional activities and, more importantly, give a synopsis of each play for those of us who need a little "help."

TEN As mentioned, there are numbered porta-potties, with Bard volunteers directing patrons to the vacant ones to ensure a quick turnaround.

ELEVEN Varied food alternatives, including wine, beer, Starbucks coffee, and other options, many of which are unique to Bard, such as Bard chocolate and Bard popcorn.

TWELVE There are few bugs. Other Shakespeare festivals performed across Canada suffer from insects. Bard, luckily, does not.

THIRTEEN "In a Nutshell" talks prior to the performances given by Riotous Youth interns (see Act V). These short (five- to seven-minute) presentations take place prior to every performance and give background to patrons on the play they are about to see.

FOURTEEN Talkback Tuesdays. On both stages, following the performances, actors answer questions from patrons and provide intimate insight into the performance and the work.

FIFTEEN Bard-B-Q and Fireworks. Prior to the Fireworks display, which occurs each year in Vancouver on three separate nights, patrons can see a play, have a wild Pacific salmon barbecue dinner, and then watch the Celebration of Light fireworks display from a private viewing area.

SIXTEEN Wine Wednesdays. On three dates, patrons can register for a pre-show wine tasting presented by special guests in the Marquee

tent and learn tasting etiquette and sample BC wines.

Performances take place every night, with the exception of Mondays when the venue is used for other events, including four offerings of Opera and Arias, a collaboration between the University of British Columbia Opera Ensemble and Vancouver Opera Orchestra. Other events on the BMO Mainstage include the Vancouver Symphony Orchestra, performing on two occasions, and Chor Leoni, the award-winning Vancouver men's choir, on four occasions.

Bard does not take itself too seriously. Despite offering classical Shakespearean theatre, the environment is devoid of any airs, and productions are completely welcoming. While some patrons do dress smartly, the vast majority are very casually attired. This is theatre for the common man (and woman)—exactly the way Shakespeare intended it to be. This accessibility trait is one of the reasons Bard has managed to grow successfully. Vancouverites trust Bard. It is now an established institution, which the local population supports. It slowly and cautiously introduced Shakespeare to its audience and made it accessible, not incomprehensible. By making Shakespeare fun, understandable, and inspirational, and by viewing high-quality, dynamic productions in an unconventional environment, audiences became loyal and remain so. They are committed to returning, so Bard is destined to remain. It is now part of the fabric of Vancouver in the summer. "Bard is my 'go-to' happy place," shared one volunteer. "Whether I am there as a patron or as a volunteer, the experience captures me. When I leave the site, I am fulfilled and richer for my participation."

[S C E N E   I I I]

Behind the Scenes

"When I was at home, I was in a better place, but travellers must be content." AS YOU LIKE IT

Toward the end of the 2015 Bard season, the Operations Manager gave me an extensive tour of the Village site. (Backstage tours are available to the public who are Bard members.) Having attended numerous productions over twenty-seven years, I was well acquainted with the public areas, but behind the scenes of the public arena was an environment I had not anticipated. I had, of course, seen actors run onto the Mainstage and disappear behind the back of the stage. What I had not expected, or even imagined, was the wonderful environment behind the Mainstage. There was a garden, complete with potted plants, picnic tables and chairs, and a shady grotto under the branches of a tree. Up along every tent guide-rope grew runner beans, with either red flowers or the pods hanging among the heavy green leaves. Each year, actor Jennifer Lines plants and tends these vegetables. Consequently, the area provides a gentle, delightful environment in which to relax (if the weather is good). When I praised Jennifer for her efforts, she told me about the problems they had faced when there was a water shortage. She then told me about the

other actors with horticulture experience who had helped and educated her with their gardening knowledge. Clearly, Bard actors are learning more than their lines in this environment.

Adjacent to this temporary garden, there is a tent for the actors. The green room (where actors wait before they appear onstage) contains large black couches, coffee tables, tea- and coffee-making facilities, and a screen showing the production so the cast know when they will be needed onstage. I was taken aback to see two industrial-sized washing machines and dryers. Having not expected laundry to be undertaken on-site, I learned it is a task conducted by the wardrobe assistants. Huge plastic containers to collect the grey water, which has to be pumped out every three days, were positioned outside the actors' tent. As a member of the management team remarked, "Everyone forgets it's in a park. There are teams that put it all together, and that's everything—fridges being lifted, which we have to run power lines to, washing machines, and in the off season, it's a field and there is nothing there."

The smaller Douglas Campbell Theatre also had its own garden, with plants supplied

> *Landscaping the village site, getting ready for the new season.*

TOP LEFT ❯ *Yuko McCulloch and Jennifer Gaze.*

TOP RIGHT ❯ *Yuko McCulloch, Matthew Rhodes, and John McCulloch.*

in 2015 by one of the actors' mother, who worked in a garden centre. Green beans were growing up all the tent ropes here as well, including the dressing-room area. Although smaller, the space was fashioned much like the other larger one. There was also a large tent dedicated to maintenance, and numerous large containers for recycling.

I was not alone in my discovery of just how much goes on behind the scenes. One Board member said, "I am almost embarrassed to confess a complete naiveté over the infrastructure. As a long-term patron, I did not see or even consider this. What makes this oversight even more remarkable is the realization that everything has to be brought on to the site, plugged in, erected, wired, secured, and constructed on a grassy field. If it is a particularly wet April and trenches need to be dug, the site can resemble a First World War battlefield."

Weather challenges were also mentioned by another Board member: "Some years, we are putting up a tent and it's beautifully sunny weather and it all goes up great. Other times, there is the wind and it's blowing ninety miles per hour,

and it's torrential rain and the trucks are getting stuck in six inches of mud, and then someone tells you we're 50 percent over budget [for] putting up the tent."

In 2015 there was a huge gale, which, although it had been forecast, still caused stress. "We had that massive windstorm that summer and I'm really grateful we had the expertise," recalled a member of the management team. "I was there and I definitely thought back to the inspections we have every year with the architects to ensure those tents are secure and sound and can withstand wind and weather."

The Village has to be protected not only from the elements but also the creatures, including rats, skunks, raccoons, crows, mice, squirrels, geese, ducks, and eagles, to name but a few. At the same time, Bard has to ensure there is no damage to parkland space. It has to work and function for four months then be dismantled, removed, and stored ready for the next season—leaving no footprint.

"That's the part which people don't think about," a member of management explained. "We incur so much grey water, it's expensive to remove, and to remove it in an environmentally sound way, as we do, it's also very labour intensive. It takes up a big footprint on the site. We need to have areas we can store it until we can remove it. It's a thing nobody thinks about."

The logistics of creating an outdoor theatre experience for over a thousand people per night for a four-month period by a not-for-profit theatre group—complying with safety, fire, and construction codes required by various government bodies, passing inspection by a team of engineers— is something I doubt many of us consider when we see actors walk confidently onto the stage in their wonderful attire. I certainly did not. Operating an arts organization in a stable building with established dressing rooms, toilets, corridors, solid floors, and a permanent stage is difficult enough. Add the complication of creating this outside, and it becomes fascinating.

As one Board member remarked, "Infrastructure is huge. Part of the funding campaign was to put in some permanent hydro connection, as they had been running power cords for years—and all that stuff you don't think about because it is just there. But we are building this artificial city and then taking it down, and then everyone wants the site pristine for the wintertime."

At the end of October each year, Bard's Production Manager meets with a Park Board official to go over the site and ensure it has been left in an acceptable condition. Just as if you had rented out your house to someone, the City of Vancouver needs the property to be returned in the same state.

[SCENE IV]

Here and Gone

"To be or not to be, that is the question."
HAMLET

As so many have discovered, there is something completely magical about watching Shakespeare in a tent, where one can look beyond the stage and see in the distance a nest of bald eagles, or a "booze cruise" party boat, or yachts decked out in lights, that can easily distract patrons from Bottom's capers, Othello's musing, or Romeo's poetry. Everyone's mind wanders during a live performance. In a traditional darkened setting, there are few options but to look at the stage itself. But Bard offers an alternative. With Bard, patrons are free to study the audience, watch the setting sun, hear the rain beat on the tent, and listen to the sound of motor-boats or the squawk of Canada geese. For years, the most famous view was of bald eagles nesting in an adjacent tree; they are still there. One of the real attractions to Bard on the Beach is the unique waterfront setting in Vanier Park. Walking across the grass to the venue in heels while trying to avoid the Canada geese droppings is a novel start to any theatre experience. Seeing the colourful tents ringed in the distinct-ive Bard Village is an attraction to regulars and newcomers alike and has been mar-keted to tourists and locals as part of the

characteristic Bard brand. The architecture reflects the pioneering days of the country, when the only opportunity Canadians had to see theatre was through moving troupes performing in tents. Attending Bard cannot be compared to attending other theatres. It is an event, a one-off, a festival to be celebrated. It is unique.

"It's like Brigadoon," remarked one actor. "It's here and it's gone, and it's actually a perfect metaphor for theatre as an art form, because you come in as an audience member . . . this event happens, and at the end of it, it's gone. The actors go back to the dressing room, they take off their stuff, they're gone. It's not permanent . . . Bard has become a cultural institution and yet, physically, it's only there for a short period."

When I asked interviewees what they liked best and least about Bard, the responses were often the same. The constant challenge was the unpredictable and frequently wet, cold weather. While most acknowledged

global warming was having an effect and the summers were warmer, most actors, volunteers, Board members, and managers articulated, using their own vernacular, the challenges of working outside in the cold. "Sometimes it's so wet and so dreary and so, so cold," remarked one actor/director. "It's like camping."

At the same time, when the temperatures are warm and the sun shines, the joys of operating a theatre on the banks of the ocean, with snow-capped mountains in the distance, were professed to be the best part of the enterprise.

Bard, like some Canadians, has two homes. It is the proud (joint) occupant of a new permanent office and production space, but each year opens up its "cottage" equivalent. In the spring, Bard undertakes the preliminary work necessary to see that its summertime residence is welcoming to guests, then, as temperatures increase, encourages everyone to visit. It's a wonderful tradition appreciated by over 100,000 people every year. ▶

ACT IV

"Are you sure that we are awake? It seems to me that yet we sleep, we dream."

A MIDSUMMER NIGHT'S DREAM

The PLAYERS

The Company

"I bear a charmed life." MACBETH

In the early 1990s, while attending exercise classes at the local community centre in East Vancouver several times a week, I met a couple of young actors, one of them a tall woman with striking red hair, who was interested in theatre. While we didn't become close friends, we shared confidences and I was often privy to their audition plights. Years later, I was delighted to see my tall, red-headed exercise friend, Colleen Wheeler, walk confidently out onto the Bard stage with commanding presence. Over the course of the last fifteen years, Colleen has been recognized as one of the most talented actors at Bard. Her iconic performances include Kate in *The Taming of the Shrew* and Elizabeth I in *Elizabeth Rex*, a role she shaved her head for. She is also remembered for shaking the head of Christopher Gaze into her bosom nightly for four months, in her role as Adriana in the 2009 production of *The Comedy of Errors* (after first checking with his wife, Jennifer, who gave her blessing).

There are a vast number of extremely talented actors and technicians who received their initial break at Bard. During the course of the interviews, actors themselves and others repeatedly

^ *Bard performance on the top of Grouse Mountain, 1995.*

described how their lives and careers had been changed because of the opportunities offered at Bard, often specifically through Christopher's keen interest in their abilities. "He has formed who I am as an actor," said one. "He goes beyond the institutional sense. He is a father figure." Another shared, "Christopher adores actors. He's grateful to us, and he adores being in the rehearsal hall and talking to actors and being an actor. He loves the old stories. There is a romantic notion that is always sprinkled in our productions because of him."

Another described the impact of Christopher's generosity on his career. "I know I wouldn't be where I am today without Christopher... he's the champion of so many people, actors, directors, designers."

And he is generous in other ways. One actor recalled a time when a short-term loan was needed to complete the purchase of a new house. When Christopher heard that the actor's immediate family were reluctant to provide this financial bridge, he stepped in to lend the money. "So he's more than a colleague or an Artistic Director—he's a really good friend."

As the Artistic Director, Christopher decides which four plays will be produced each year. This task is done in consultation with a number of individuals, including

actors, designers, theatre academics, and directors, whom Christopher uses as a sounding board to inform his deliberations. As one actor/director shared, Bard tries to maintain a span of five to six years before a production is repeated. Christopher has a felt board in his office on which he moves around cards with plays written on them to map out a five-year plan.

A Midsummer Night's Dream, *2014*.

Directors are booked a year or more in advance of a performance, so for productions scheduled for 2017, Christopher would have begun approaching likely candidates up to eighteen months earlier, in 2016 (see Appendices). The pre-production development stage presents a huge artistic challenge for any director—they have to think of their concept, refine it, present it to the Artistic Director, maybe refine it again, and then, if it is accepted, start the work of developing the concept. Pitches are received from directors who are known to Christopher, as well as from those he is not well acquainted with.

One Bard volunteer, in commenting on how many directors like working with Christopher, recounted one director's experience. "He wanted to do a play and Christopher said, 'That's great.' Then he suggested something more, a bit more risky, and Christopher said, 'Wonderful, wonderful.' And then he takes it a step

further, and he still gets Christopher's full support and encouragement. The director thought he'd died and gone to heaven."

In addition to finding the right directors and establishing a balance of performances, consideration must be given to the two productions that will be sharing the same stage. As two different plays occur on the BMO Mainstage and two on the Howard Family Stage on alternate nights, the logistics of changing the set after each performance and the requirements of the actors' roles (the same actors are employed on each stage) need to be addressed. Plays must be rotated, with thought given to the subject matter and which plays are popular and can therefore generate a stable audience, along with those less well known. As a member of Bard management explained, "Christopher is the epicentre of decision-making over what we present. He consults widely and enthusiastically with many people . . . he talks to actors, funders, patrons, Board members. He talks to all these people to crystalize it in his own mind. This is one tip of the iceberg. The other is to make sure the play will work, because we haven't done it for 'x' number of years, because it will work in repertory, because we have the actors, ages, gender, level of experience. The season has to have balance."

‹ A Midsummer Night's Dream, *2014*. DAVID BLUE (BARD'S PRODUCTION PHOTOGRAPHER SINCE 2000)

Bard is keen to challenge itself by extending artistic boundaries, so over the recent past has presented lesser known Shakespeare works such as *Cymbeline* and *Pericles* in addition to non-Shakespearean (but related) works, such as *Elizabeth Rex* and *Equivocation*. At time of writing, only two Shakespearean plays have not yet been performed at Bard: *Coriolanus* and *Henry VIII.*

Once the plays have been selected and the four directors are in place, auditions can be considered. Bard has always enjoyed a close relationship with two of Vancouver's leading theatre schools—Studio 58, at Langara College, and the University of British Columbia. For a number of years, Christopher has visited both institutions to audition students. A number of students have gone on to be involved in Bard after having been picked directly out of theatre school for general auditions and then cast to plays. As one member of the management team explained, "A lot of students got their initial break at Bard."

The first stage in the process of becoming a Bard actor is the general audition. These are advertised to the artistic community through emails, social media, the Canadian Actors' Equity Association website (caea. com), and community organizations and on the Bard website. Bard asks for two contrasting Shakespearean monologues (a maximum of two minutes per speech) and a thirty-second song, as a number of Bard productions involve singing. General auditions take place in June and July and are usually geared toward the actors Bard is unacquainted with or who have previous experience at Bard but are returning after a period of absence. It is a way to establish the talent available. Surprisingly, at this stage, the actors may not know which play they are auditioning for.

During my interviews, I was told the delightful story of one young girl who saw Bard's production of *A Midsummer Night's Dream* in 1999 and subsequently decided to become an actor. Over the course of the next few years, she pursued this ambition and in 2014 appeared as Helena in that play, wearing the same costume as was used in the 1999 production she originally fell in love with.

The next stage is the casting auditions, which take place in July and August. These are attended by the directors. Sometimes directors, if available, are included in the general auditions, but many work in other cities, so this is not always possible. The two directors who are sharing either the BMO Mainstage or the Howard Family Stage are always involved in this process. It is not unusual for actors already involved in Bard's current season to be under consideration for a forthcoming one. This process used to take place after the season ended, but Bard found it was losing out on some talented actors who by that time had booked jobs elsewhere, so the process was moved forward.

TOP ❯ Falstaff, *2010.*

BOTTOM ❯ Henry V, *2010.*

For casting auditions, actors are given a specific piece to prepare a couple of weeks in advance of the audition. At the audition appointment, each actor is greeted outside the audition room and then taken in to be introduced to the panel, which includes the Artistic Director, often the Associate Artistic Director, and the two other directors. The panel speaks with the actor for a while, a member of the management team explained, "to get a sense of who they are, where they are coming from, and hopefully get rid of some of their nerves and let them know they are here to succeed."

Bard (and particularly Christopher) has a reputation for being very generous to nervous actors. "He made me feel good," shared one actor/director. "You know, usually . . . well, you don't always get to feel good. It's something I consider when I'm directing . . . what I can do to make this actor feel better about what they're doing."

The directors are often looking for something specific, and sometimes actors are called back if, for example, a director needs to see whether an actor will complement another actor. Delivery is carefully considered, as explained by Christopher in an interview with *Vancouver Magazine* in 2011. "I enjoy actors who are well trained, are well centered, and deliver clear, inspired performances. That excites me. I'm getting

< Macbeth, *2012.* THE 2012 MAINSTAGE COMPANY

more and more particular the older I get. I am focused on the way they stream words together, and whether I can hear them or not. I don't just mean hear sound, but hear definition of words."

After casting is complete, the directors, in consultation with the Artistic Director, have to decide who they want for each role. Shakespeare generally has more male than female roles, so, as one actress told me, the competition is very tough for female actors and the pool of talent huge. Sometimes difficulties arise when two radically different plays—for example, a tragedy and a comedy—are sharing the same stage, requiring two different skill sets. Some actors can undertake both genres, others cannot. And it is not only the subject matter that has to be considered. As Bard has a very long season, attempts are made to not cast the same actor in two leading roles. While Bard does offer support for actors during the season, such as voice coaches, the directors are cognizant of the fact that two leading, demanding roles are difficult to maintain over six months.

Once the list has been finalized, Christopher calls the successful actors to offer them a part. For many, this is a huge accolade, not only for their resumé but financially. It was mentioned to me on numerous occasions that Bard offers one of the longest contracts in Western Canada. A Bard contract is recognized as beneficial, and therefore highly sought after, not only because of the stable, secure income provided, but also because actors can form a collegial group, even though they may be exhausted at the end of the season.

I was told that current Bard actors who have been offered a future part may feel reluctant to discuss it, as they may not know whether colleagues currently sharing the same stage have been granted roles in the forthcoming season. While rejection is common within the profession, and it is the unfortunate nature of the beast, the actors within the Bard community are professional, and unsuccessful applicants are happy for their colleagues.

In such a long contract, with the actors working in close confines for six months, the ensemble being created has to bond. They must form a rapport not only onstage but offstage. Christopher must choose actors not only for their artistic abilities but with the health of the entire Company in mind. As recounted in Act II, in 1992 there was an actor who fractionalized the Company, resulting in tensions that were not overcome until the season ended, something Christopher still vividly recalls over twenty years later. Other theatre companies have much shorter seasons, so if there are conflicts, they are short-lived and can be tolerated. With Bard's long season, it is imperative to have good interpersonal relationships between cast members and technical crew. The long contract could potentially be a nightmare if the right people are not hired.

While some actors who are offered contracts have to check with agents or consult schedules, most say yes immediately and are sent a contract. Bard does not use understudies, so when a crisis happens —such as the time an actor was hit by a vehicle while cycling to work and suffered a broken leg, or when another actor suffered a slipped disc on the morning of opening night—all must adapt to ensure the performance is not jeopardized. In the slipped disc incident, the Board Chair (a renowned sports-medicine physician) used his contacts with the highly qualified Vancouver Whitecaps soccer team physiotherapist. This specialist agreed to provide treatment in the soccer team's dressing room, enabling the actor to perform on opening night while a long-term contingency plan could be formulated. This unfortunate event provides an example of how the whole organization has to work together in times of crisis—the Board Chair who sat in the audience on opening night with his medical bag under his seat, ready to leap into action if required; the Director and Artistic Director who needed to rearrange and reassign roles for subsequent performances; the actors who had to quickly learn new lines and roles; and the stage managers who needed to prompt and support the cast.

In the early days, the search for actors was limited to BC (in one of the first Annual Reports Christopher commented there was no need to look farther afield, as the talent pool in Western Canada was so large). Now he often takes colleagues to Eastern Canada to seek new talent. And

▲ Hamlet, *2013.* THE 2013 MAINSTAGE COMPANY

as Bard's reputation has grown, so has the number of actors who would like to appear in the tents.

Christopher's interpretation of Shakespeare has also evolved. "When you look at the Annual Reports and my comments, you will find I say things like 'You'll never see a production of people in modern dress' and things like that, and I'm completely contradicting myself. I've grown, and that is the essence of Bard. I have grown as our audience has grown. My growth has been with the audience. We have matched each other."

Bard is imaginative but also strongly traditional. The text is respected with clear delivery of the words, a priority for Christopher and the directors he supports, thereby preserving the essence of Shakespeare, while at the same time offering innovative interpretations.

Rehearsals take place in April from 10 AM to 6 PM and are staggered between productions. Once a performance starts, actors may be rehearsing during the day and performing in the evenings. This is the most intense time. When both shows sharing the same stage start and the full performance schedule is in place, the actors are then focused on the evening performances and daytime pressure is eliminated.

In contrast to some theatre companies, Bard is known for giving actors time to learn, understand, and appreciate the words they are tasked to deliver. "There is more time to sit and talk about what you are doing and what you are saying," shared one actor. "At the first table read, you look at what is happening in each scene and get time to learn and say, 'Yes, I get it.'" Bard is also known for how well its actors are treated. "Bard has a lot of respect for its actors; it tries to accommodate us in so many ways," said another actor. "And it's Christopher's influence. He makes people happy and he treats us all, everyone, with respect."

Prior to rehearsals, Bard offers an optional, three-day, paid training workshop, which, as one of the less-experienced actors told me, is really beneficial and almost unique to Bard. "It starts three days before the table read. You get to meet people you'll be working with in the next five months . . . you do really silly acting exercises, all the things you did in college. It's a bonding experience. You get to feel super comfortable with everyone before rehearsals start; it's not like other places."

This unique bond is fostered backstage between the actors throughout the season, as one Board member said. "Elsewhere, it can be very business-like: do the play, go offstage, take off your makeup, get dressed, go home. Here, you do the play, go backstage, have a beer, sit down on the couches, and you become a family. Of course, it is very West Coast—it's Bard reflecting the West Coast and BC."

A lovely example of this bond occurred in 2015, when the actors on the Howard Family Stage invited those from the BMO Mainstage out on a prom night. They bought corsages and escorted them to the venue. A couple of actors even got married on the Bard stage. As a fellow actor described, "It was beautiful—just as they were saying their vows, two swallows came in." After performances, games are often played, and whisky ("because you don't have to refrigerate it") is occasionally consumed. Recalled one young actor about his nerve-wracking first day at Bard and his apprehension about being among what he described as "real" actors, "It was very much like that first day at school, but it felt so welcoming and warm and safe, and just unbelievably good."

Of course, it is not *all* fantastic. There are drawbacks. There is no "time off" during the performance season, which has eight performances per week. "I missed my mum and dad's fiftieth wedding anniversary," explained one actor. "I missed my brother's wedding. There are big life events that happen in the summertime. I've watched an actor Skype their sister's wedding, in tears, running onstage, then running back off to see more. People make a lot of sacrifices. But you cannot say no to six months of work for one day."

Another actor commented on the challenges of working six nights a week over the summer when a young family is involved, missing out on family summer vacations because the contract is "a blessing and a curse." For this reason, many actors who have been with Bard a number of years take a year off to enjoy the season and subsequently return.

Some actors transition from actors to directors. Not all make this change, nor want to, but Christopher and others within the Bard family (specifically Douglas Campbell before he passed away), have encouraged those with the ability to develop this craft. One actor shared how Christopher had been a "great personal champion" for him, encouraging him as a director and giving him his first large theatre production opportunity. "I never pushed him for that, he just decided."

While audience members are focused mainly on the actors, a number of other highly skilled individuals are involved in the productions behind the scenes. These individuals have roles that are often not recognized by those watching the plays. Bard's Production Manager, for example, selects the stage managers, technicians, and lighting technicians. Anything to do with design—set, costume, lighting, and sound—is the responsibility of the directors, usually in consultation with the Artistic Director.

Once the director has been selected and his or her interpretation has been discussed with and approved by the Artistic Director, the choice of costume and set designers must then be made. Set designers, technicians, and costume designers are sometimes recruited from theatre schools in the same way actors are. One set designer described her role to me as taking the words from the page and creating a visual environment. "I'm there to support the script first, the director second, the Company's vision or budget line third, and finally my artistic vision."

A director may request the set designer they want to work with, based on the period or genre to be created, to set (for example), *The Taming of the Shrew* in the Wild West, or *Love's Labour's Lost* in the 1930s. The challenge for the director and set designer is, of course, the staging of two productions on the same stage. The same set designer is assigned to work on both plays. Although consultation between the two directors and the set designer should theoretically take place in October and November the year prior to the performances, this is not always possible in a face-to-face forum, so pitches and concepts have to be sent by the designer to the director to be developed.

By January, a concrete design begins to emerge. A model is built as a blueprint for the carpenters to work from, to ensure it is feasible, affordable, and meets requirements. Construction takes place at a University of British Columbia construction shop in April. The set is put in position once the tent is in place.

As the set is approved, props and furnishings must also be considered. This encompasses a broad spectrum, from decisions over the fabric needed to cover a chaise longue to the swords, fans, and musical instruments required during the production. Once the production is up and running, the set designer's main tasks are

over; however, they are often involved in the rehearsals. "I try to attend as many rehearsals as possible, again to support the directors and to support the cast," said one designer. "Through their exploration they may say, 'Oh, we need a bench; we can't sit on the floor.' But it is tricky, as you can't be there all the time."

When I asked about the performances themselves, a set designer confessed: "As a designer, you see it too often and all you see are the things you want to change. You sit there and think, 'I should have done that, I could have done that.' As a designer, it is difficult to sit through your work."

In addition to the set designer, another key individual in the process is the costume designer. I myself, for many years, have been in absolute awe of the costumes (and especially the shoes), and I know other audience members share my passion. What I had not anticipated is that this feeling is shared by those who wear the clothes on a nightly basis. "The costumes are amazing . . . They can make you feel so beautiful," one actor told me. "Every night, what we put on is divine. It's the way they drape the fabric on you, and they match it to you, and sometimes they are using silks and the most beautiful materials." Another commented, "I hate getting dressed up for Halloween as it is such a comedown after appearing at Bard." This is a far cry from Bard's early days when plastic children's hula hoops were used under the Elizabethan dresses because the Company could not afford under-structures. Now, as one designer explained, "We are building all the underwear from scratch the proper way."

For a long time, Bard combined the role of Head of Wardrobe (the individual charged with making the costumes) with that of the Costume Designer (the individual responsible for the design), but as Bard grew, these functions were separated.

The Costume Designer is chosen by the director, after deciding the era in which the play will be set—for example, in the American Civil War, or in the 1960s. The designer then needs to research various designs appropriate for the time, which can sometimes take months. "Every process is different," said one designer. "Often you research from scratch, so you get sidetracked, you look at histories, you find stuff out, that may only have slight relevance, but once you have ideas, you sit down and start sketching."

Costume designers, like set designers, directors, and actors, are employed under seasonal contracts. Many have long histories of working at Bard and toil long hours to ensure the best is created. (Bard Artistic Associate Mara Gottler has been involved in over seventy Bard productions.) These designers work to a deadline and can spend weeks researching and sketching before drawing and painting the designs. They also design the shoes and hairstyles.

Throughout this process, the other key individual is the Head of Wardrobe. This individual is responsible for coordinating the realization of the costume designs, within the allocated budget. There is a Head of Wardrobe, an Assistant Head of Wardrobe, and up to four different designers.

Anyone who has seen a Bard production cannot help but be highly impressed by the quality and effect the garments have in enhancing performances. Frequently, the movement and dialogue onstage can take second place, as audience members gaze in awe at the gowns, uniforms, cloaks, and shoes.

Bard's extensive costume collection, including garments from its twenty-eight years of productions, was recently enlarged by a number of costumes from the Vancouver Playhouse. The generous donation came from Paul and Darlene Howard, who acquired the costumes after the Playhouse closed. While Bard now has an extensive wardrobe to draw upon, this was not always the case. Bard's first production of *King Lear*, with Alan Scarfe directing, demanded lavish dresses that the designer could not create within the allocated budget. Bard flew the designer to the Stratford Festival in Ontario to look into the possibility of renting costumes, but when rental, cleaning, and shipping costs were all considered, it was still outside the budget. "It was Christopher who said, 'You've got to pitch it to the Board and explain to them,'" the designer explained. "And, God love them, I think they gave us twice the budget and that allowed us to build."

As the costume design is finalized, the Costume Designer works with the Head of Wardrobe, who helps determine which garments need to be built from scratch, which can be revised from existing costumes, and which are already available in stock. Once there is an approved design, the build starts. There are multiple teams, each led by a cutter who works with the designer to interpret the costume sketches and draft and drape the patterns for the garments, explained a member of Bard management. "This is a highly creative and technical job that requires years of training and experience. They are assisted by a first hand, an experienced stitcher who has often worked with the cutter for many years, and a team of one or more other stitchers, who are all responsible for the sewing and construction of the garments. All of these are highly skilled freelance contractors, in demand in theatre and film, but most come back to Bard, year after year, some for as many as twenty-five years."

Sometimes as many as 50 percent of the costumes seen in one season have been used in some form in previous productions. One designer commented, "We are not Cirque du Soleil—we operate on very tight budgets." A considerable amount of reuse takes place, especially in a show that involves a number of costume changes. Folklore tells of Bard patrons, volunteers, and other Bard "groupies" who delight in identifying costumes from previous seasons.

Within the theatre community, it is common practice to rent costumes from other companies, but Bard tends not to do this, because the long season takes a tremendous toll on the garments, depending on the physicality of the role. However, Bard does rent its costumes to other theatre groups.

The Head of Wardrobe is also responsible for hiring dressers who work backstage with the actors, a role that was described to me as a combination of "dressing and camping." Their job is to facilitate quick changes and help dress actors in hard-to-put-on period garments, as well as care for, launder, and repair the costumes and wigs throughout the run of the show. However, they are not the only ones with an eye on the wear and tear on the costumes. Actors are also responsible for looking after their costumes, explained one actor. "I always keep a very close eye on my costume, as if there is a little snag in the hem, particularly at Bard with all those stairs, if a heel gets stuck, you can go head over heels. I did that in my first year ... got my heel stuck in the hem of my dress and I stumbled down the stairs; the audience laughed—they thought it was intentional—but it wasn't."

Getting dressed for a Bard appearance can take a considerable period of time. While actors are only required to arrive thirty minutes before curtain, many come well in advance. Makeup and "getting into corsets," in particular, take time. The confines of a tight corset, full body armour, or heavy chain mail can make it difficult to bend down to lace up shoes. Going to the washroom also becomes a logistical challenge. Tight corsets can affect voice delivery, so actors wearing them often have to amend delivery once dress rehearsals start.

Bard's costume department is sensitive to the needs of its performers. When Colleen Wheeler was pregnant and playing Adriana in *The Comedy of Errors*, ice packs were built into her dresses to keep her cool (she gave birth the day after her final stage performance, after one of the backstage staff advised a lot of vigorous dancing during her final performance to "shake that baby out"). It is questionable whether many other theatre companies would have been this accommodating.

While Bard draws from the bank of talented backstage professionals it has become well acquainted with over the years, it also offers opportunities to young, newly emerging talent in the industry through involvement with local theatre schools. For the four shows, the design and production staff includes two lighting designers, four sound designers, four costume designers, and two set designers, who, according to a member of the management team, "have either worked for us before, or are new and very experienced." After operating for almost thirty years, Bard has created and nurtured a huge talent pool. This pool continues to grow.

Again I wonder how many audience members, during those wonderful, warm summer evenings, enjoying their Bard chocolate and glass of wine while engaged in a highly entertaining production, think about the considerable time, numerous logistics, and multitude of people involved in the creation and delivery of the four plays offered each season at Bard.

As one Board member remarked, "It's quite a remarkable process, from the day the play is decided upon to Opening Night. Most of us do not get a sense of this, or of the artistic process."

[S C E N E   I I]

Management

"Some are born great, some achieve greatness, and some have greatness thrust upon them." TWELFTH NIGHT

In addition to the actors, designers, and directors who work on part-time contracts, there are a number of full-time staff who are tasked with keeping the wheels of Bard turning throughout the year. While the public face of Bard is very seasonal, for a four-month period, a professional team is working fifty-two weeks a year ensuring productions successfully unfold during the summer months. What I found striking about this group of senior management is that it is composed almost entirely of women. As mentioned earlier, during the course of this research, a couple of male respondents commented on Christopher's and Claire's ability to identify confident, capable women, which was evident when I spoke to these women. While a few members of the management team have been with Bard for over ten years, most were recruited within the last five years, including a couple of long-term employees who have risen from junior administrative to management positions.

In 2015, Bard had a full-time staff of twenty, including the Artistic Director and Executive Director. Senior management roles (all, with the exception of one, staffed by women) include a Senior Development Manager, responsible for fundraising, donors, sponsorship; Operations Director, responsible for everything "front of house"–volunteers, security, concession, and boutique; Director of Marketing and Communications, responsible for telling the Bard story to many different constituencies, publicity, public relations, and all promotional activities and ticket sales; Production Manager; and Director of Finance. There is also a Director of Education, responsible for Bard's educational component (see Act V).

Bard hires over two hundred part-time and seasonal staff, thereby making a significant contribution as a local employer. As the second-largest theatre company in British Columbia and ninth-largest in Canada, Bard is responsible for $3.8 million in local wages (2016 figures), employing 264 artists, technicians, and administrators annually. Most report through the management team to the Executive Director (see Appendices).

The reconfiguration of the management structure in 2013 was a positive game-changer in the life of Bard. While a couple of the current management team members felt apprehensive about receiving promotions, all embraced the challenge and received support so that, two years later, they professed contentment and confidence in these positions. The shakeup was the result of the Board appointing an interim Managing Director

138

(as shown in Act II, the Chair of the Board stepped down to take on this role) before the arrival of Claire Sakaki, the current Executive Director.

When remarking on the changes that had been made by the interim Managing Director, Claire saw the fact that he came from a different industry as being

a really positive influence on the organization. He didn't come at change or growth from the perspective of what a theatre would normally do, or what a not-for-profit would normally do; he came at it from what he would do as a business person in any industry, and I think he made some fantastic changes that I don't know if a lot of people would have had the guts to make. He really did some out-of-the-box thinking. For example, he restructured the administration staff and changed portfolios quite drastically. He pulled apart other jobs and promoted people, sometimes across boundaries, so someone who was in marketing moved to operations, and it was brilliant. All I know is that when I arrived, these people had been in these positions for about a year and they were thriving.

The few employees who have been with Bard over ten years all commented positively on its recent growth. As one member of management remarked, "Changed? It *has* changed. I almost cannot answer the question, it's changed so much. We went from year-round staff of four or five to fifteen to twenty. We've grown and we've created an incredible, devoted team working year-round."

This management group is now enjoying a brand-new, state-of-the-art work environment. I spent a few days within this space reading twenty-five years of Bard Annual Reports (which I doubt no one else had ever asked to see nor will ask to see again) in the library/meeting room close to the reception. In this glass-walled space, I could be easily seen, and during the course of my time there, I was treated as "one of the team." Bard staff at every level—from the volunteer at the reception desk to the management staff I met and interviewed—came in to chat, ask if I needed anything, and inquire how the writing was going. When I was conducting interviews, my subjects' colleagues would often stop in and be introduced. Christopher and Claire both made a point of stopping in whenever they saw me. I was made to feel very welcome and completely at home. But I was also a fly on the wall for the humorous banter often occurring in the kitchen area, just down the hall from where I was working. Social scientists often use what are termed "unobtrusive methods" to collect data—the quiet observation of practices, employed to gain additional insight into subjects under analysis. My time in the Bard office certainly provided more first-hand evidence of this organization's unique culture and the open, happy "family atmosphere" so many had commented on.

[SCENE III]

Volunteers

"You speedy helpers that ... appear and aid me in this enterprise."

HENRY VI, PART I

Throughout the course of the eight months I spent collecting data for this book, it was evident that one sentiment was constant among everyone within and connected to Bard: appreciation for the volunteers.

At the Bard Village entrance, tickets are dispensed from paid box-office staff, and there are paid managers in each department, but from that point onward it appears the rest of the Village is operated by a team of very happy, accomplished, helpful, red-vested volunteers who take tickets, show patrons to their seats, convey information, answer questions, sell food and beverages, staff the boutique shop, and work at special events such as private and corporate hospitality functions. They also shepherd up to one thousand patrons (from the two theatres) during the twenty-minute intermission to the porta-potties to ensure a quick turnaround. There seems to be no task undertaken without confidence and delight.

Almost 250 volunteers work at Bard over the summer months, with the

TOP ⌃ *Dina Sudlow, Stacey Menzies (Operations Manager), Shivani Seth, Terri Jelic, and Deb Pound.*

BOTTOM ⌃ *Audrey Zaharichuk.*

minimum time commitment being twenty-five hours, totalling over 28,000 hours annually. "Oh, you get caught up in it. I wasn't going to do one hundred hours, but it is so easy to do," commented a retired female volunteer. Indeed, most offer to dedicate far more of their time to the organization than the required number. Bard has always used volunteers. In the very early days, they were friends and relatives of the actors, only twenty-five in total, who worked a much shorter five-week season. Now Bard employs a full-time, salaried Volunteer Manager for their administration.

Each year, approximately 150 to 170 volunteers who previously worked at Bard return for an another season. Over fifty volunteers have ten or more years of experience, and ten of these have been volunteers for over twenty years. Volunteers also contribute financially to Bard's educational programs by donating the tips received when working at the concession to this initiative (see Act V). They are kept informed by a regularly emailed newsletter providing updates on what is happening within the Bard community. Bard also uses its own website and social media to attract interest, but it appears there have never been any issues with the recruitment and retention of volunteers. "We rarely don't get enough interest," confirmed one member of management, adding that each season they receive about another hundred applications. "We don't have any [recruitment problems]. So much a part of Bard is this retention of volunteers—they do it and come back year after year."

During January and February, volunteers who worked previous seasons are asked by email if they would like to return. New applicants are invited to an orientation, which explains everything involved, and where prospective volunteers meet returning volunteers, thereby establishing a type of mentorship initiative and building upon the Bard family experience. Each new prospective volunteer is interviewed, and there is also an established procedure for returning volunteers, including an orientation about the forthcoming season and the option to take refresher training if they desire.

Volunteers are employed in the following capacities.

CONCESSION
(front of counter and assistant)

The older volunteers tend to undertake the front-of-counter tasks, taking orders and payments, while the younger ones (including those under nineteen who are too young to serve alcohol) work behind the counter to retrieve ice cream, coffee, and non-alcoholic drinks. Great rapport seems to be established in this paired relationship, which can see intense activity during the twenty-minute intermissions. After intermissions are over, volunteers clean up and leave at approximately 9 PM. During the first part of the per-

formance, volunteers gather and jovially gossip among themselves. It reminded me of high school recess period, complete with stories, teasing, and a lot of laughter. "I like working concession," remarked one volunteer. "You never get bored. If working as an usher, you see the same play; at the concession, it's lots of different people."

USHERS

These individuals work in the theatres, attending all the performances, showing patrons to their seats and clearing up afterwards. This position involves the longest time commitment, but offers the advantage of being able to watch the performance. One volunteer, who has been

ABOVE LEFT ▲ *Jane Harrison, Jo-Ann Ternier, and Beth Harper.*

ushering for the past seven years, commented on why it's a preferred position. "I really like the interacting with patrons, helping them with anything that needs doing or answering their questions. Ninety-five percent of Bard patrons are really nice people, just sweethearts."

GREETERS AND TICKET TAKERS

These volunteers work outside the Bard Village, guiding patrons to the ticket booths, taking tickets, and assisting with patrons' questions once they are in the Village. "The role I enjoy most is Village greeting," shared one volunteer. "You interact with the patrons as they arrive, usually in a happy mood, to join in the celebration of great plays and acting."

AUDIENCE SERVICES

These volunteers are particularly knowledgeable about the Bard organization and can answer questions about becoming a donor, the Bard season, where the washrooms are located, and basically anything else a patron may ask. One female volunteer proudly recalled a smartly dressed Japanese businessman who asked her out for dinner after she successfully answered his inquiries. She declined his offer. "I think the Ask Us [Audience Services], where one presents the face of Bard to the public, is the best role," explained one volunteer. "It provides an opportunity to engage with patrons in numerous ways and is truly a major PR position. We answer all sorts of questions—everything from 'Where's the washroom?' to 'What is this play about?' We help patrons navigate the site, get taxis, learn the history of Bard, become new members, and renew memberships. We are really a major component of the Bard experience."

BOUTIQUE

Working in the Bard Boutique involves marketing and selling merchandise before the performance starts and during the intermission. The Bard Boutique has been a great success and a significant revenue generator for the Company. Personally, I love discovering the new merchandise on offer while I devour an ice cream or enjoy a glass of wine during the performance break. One volunteer described how the Boutique Manager is "always thinking, 'What can we do? What would be neat?' The past year she came up with wanting to sell the costume sketches, and I loved that. And then one night our Operations Manager said, 'Let's throw a party one night and have a boutique evening, and have the designers there and invite costume students and design students and anyone interested.'"

SPECIAL EVENTS

Volunteers help out at special private functions in the Bard Village and for additional performances and events such as Wine Wednesdays and Opera and Arias concerts. One volunteer explained their preference for this position: "I don't do concession, but I do events. I like these—I'm given clear direction but allowed a lot of freedom."

While most volunteers work only during the summer in the Bard Village itself, a few are "employed" in the Bard permanent office to offer administrative support weekday afternoons. Volunteer positions also exist out of season within this office for some clerical duties, such as special mailings, and during the Wine Festival.

GREEN TEAM

Some volunteers also register for the "Green Team." A few years ago, Jennifer Gaze recognized the Village could be enhanced by the introduction of planters. She approached a nursery, which assisted with the design and implementation. A team of volunteers also helped with this process, and others now water and care for the plants on-site. As Jennifer explained, "The Green Team volunteers maintain the plants. They have other duties, but they also look after the plants. Many of them are already fantastic gardeners. It's not uncommon to see audience members taking photographs of our flowers."

RECRUITMENT AND TRAINING

As mentioned earlier, experienced volunteers are employed to interview new volunteers, explain the scope of work, answer questions, and, in certain respects, become mentors. They introduce all new volunteers to the Bard family. One volunteer explained the appeal of being on the recruiting team: "Bard on the Beach attracts stellar volunteer applicants. It is always a privilege to meet and interview potential volunteers and, if they and we determine there is a fit, assist them to be successful in their volunteer role."

PORTA-POTTY PATROL

This is perhaps not the most desirable position, but one much needed to ensure patrons use these facilities in an efficient manner during the twenty-minute intermission period, when as many as one thousand patrons leave the two theatres. I was informed of one volunteer who is particularly adept in this role, using the cry, "Remember to lock the door. Bard wants to keep all entertainment on the stage."

In addition to Bard T-shirts and red vests (and black aprons, if working in the concession), volunteers also wear badges with their name and length of service. In 2016, volunteers received a one-dollar discount on goods purchased at the concession, free parking in July and August, and a 20 percent discount at the Bard Boutique. They can also earn complimentary seats to the performances and discount tickets for previews after completing a predetermined number of volunteer hours. A number of social events for the volunteers are organized during the year, such as a Christmas party, a Twelfth Night function, and pub nights. Different groups also get together for bridge nights and Oscar parties, and even an organized trip to see some of Bard's regular actors perform in Calgary. Just as they did in the early days, these volunteers employ initiative when the need arises. During the Women's World Cup of Soccer in 2015, other venues seemed to be monopolizing the supply of soft drinks, so Bard volunteers took it upon themselves

TOP ▲ *Audrey Zaharichuk and Christopher Gaze.*

LEFT ◄ *Karen Shimokura, Jenny McDonald, and Rati Arora.*

to access a local Safeway to ensure Bard's supplies were maintained.

Most volunteers (except ushers) are required to arrive at the Bard Village ninety minutes prior to curtain (normally 6 PM for an evening show, 12:30 PM for a matinee). Upon arrival, they attend a pre-show meeting, which provides information about the performance, patrons, and special guests who may be attending. It is also a time to convey information about Bard and additional volunteer opportunities. Ushers attend a meeting sixty minutes prior to curtain. The Bard Village opens an hour before curtain, and events such as the pre-performance Nutshell talks are scheduled prior to curtain.

Volunteer shifts run between two and five hours. Ushers stay for the duration of the performance, whereas Audience Services and Concession may leave after the intermission, when clearing up has been completed. If a performance finishes at 11 PM, it is not unusual for an usher to still be on site at 11:30 PM, sweeping up popcorn and ensuring the theatre is left clean for the following day. On Talkback Tuesdays, when actors talk to patrons after the performance, this time is extended further. Each night, twenty to thirty volunteers work at for each of the two performances.

The fact that so many volunteers return year after year is a true testament to their commitment. While there are many perks, a few downsides emerged, including the issue of parking—volunteers receive free parking in July and August but must pay in June and September. One usher also mentioned the unglamorous side of the job: "Some of the things you have to do aren't particularly sexy, like cleaning the tents after the performances. It usually isn't too bad, but sometimes you have to wonder what their homes are like after seeing all the garbage they throw on the floor."

Chasing geese is another unpleasant task, as one volunteer aptly explained: "Those gangs of grumpy avians often try to get in without a ticket and make a heck of a racket when you try to move them on. Not to mention the fact they excrete about every three minutes everywhere. I hate having to clean up bird poop."

While these downsides may be seen as minor inconveniences, in 2010 other factors arose to cause this "happy band of pilgrims" to be anything but content. A rapidly changing organizational model, the bigger tent, a move to pre-assigned seating, growing pains, and a lack of communication resulted in many feeling that their concerns were not being addressed. As volunteers had always been the lifeblood of the organization, the decision was made to recruit a Board member who had first-hand experience working as a volunteer. Now this group of 250 had a voice on the Board, and by everyone's account, any issues that were evident in the past had been addressed. If issues do arise in the future, there is now a structure in place to speak to them. As one volunteer confirmed, "They very much listened and things changed."

Volunteers, like other members of the organization, consistently mentioned the notion of family and the sense of belonging, unique to Bard, as the reason they keep returning. One spoke of feeling like part of the family and therefore an integral part of its success and longevity, and something to be proud of. Related to this is the belief that, as a group, they are thoroughly appreciated, as another volunteer explained: "Bard is extremely thoughtful and great-hearted in their acknowledgement of volunteers. The Board, Christopher, Claire, and the directors, actors, crew, and patrons all regularly take time to offer words of praise and appreciation to the volunteers. I don't question if my contribution is valued at Bard, they let me know it is."

And this affection is reciprocated. When actor Colleen Wheeler was pregnant during the 2009 performance season, volunteers gave her a baby shower complete with clothes, homemade blankets, and other gifts for the newborn. Other actors reported volunteers frequently arriving at the Village with homemade cookies and cakes to share.

During my interviews with volunteers, many of which took place during the Bard performances in the Village itself, I encountered a fantastic, eclectic group of people. I was surprised to learn that some had not seen any of the performances, and volunteered because of what they personally gained from the experience. I had presumed every volunteer was an impassioned Shakespeare fan, but this is not the case. They are just lovely individuals who like hanging out in a tent with like-minded people. As one Board member confirmed, "You will have people who will volunteer at Bard for over fifty hours a year and not see a single play. They just like the atmosphere, they like the park, they like the people."

The experience of receiving far more than was put in was expressed consistently. While most of the volunteers were older (over the age of fifty) and many retired, there were a number of younger individuals. To graduate from a British Columbia high school, students are

TOP ❯ *Company, staff, and volunteers, 2014.*

BOTTOM LEFT ❯ *Joan Ouellette.*

BOTTOM CENTRE ❯ *Meribeth Fleetham, Bard vvolunteer for more than twenty-five years, in 2011.*

BOTTOM RIGHT ❯ *Rati Arora.*

▲ *Volunteers taking part in the Polar Bard Swim.*

required to complete a number of volunteer hours, and some students obtain these at Bard. One young man, who in 2015 had completed over 260 hours volunteering, was particularly open with me. I sat with him away from the other volunteers during his break and asked about his own story. He candidly talked about having some issues "fitting in" with his high school cohort and then explained what Bard means to him. "The best part is the community, so jovial and everyone is so nice. I think because they like being here, everyone is so friendly . . . It's so much fun—so, so much fun. I love it so much . . . I can't imagine what my life would be like without it. The place changes lives. I have major anxiety, I've been depressed—this place is a solace. It warms my heart."

As I transcribe this interview, I become emotional recalling the enthusiasm and eloquence of this earnest, intelligent young man who was only eighteen, and how, when I asked what he would be doing after the season finished, he replied: "Wait for the next season to start." I am delighted to report the story does not end there. In 2016, during a dress rehearsal, I encountered this young man again and learned he was now employed by Bard on a seasonal contract.

The "best" volunteer story I was lucky enough to learn of and which is folklore within the Bard community is about a couple who met at Bard in 1999 (although half the couple stated she has no recollection of him then), when both started to volunteer just one day a week. He said, "In 2001, I met her again and we worked together for a lot of the summer. We worked fireworks, so we talked a lot about our lives and our families over the summer . . . It was during the first fireworks and we were hanging up our vests and I asked for her phone number." They fell in love and by June 2002 were an established couple who, when Christopher enquired whether they were married, retorted, "No, but we are in debt together." They married in 2005. It appears that while many Vancouverites were busy enjoying Shakespeare in a tent, romance was blossoming under the adjacent canvas concession. Sixteen years later, they continue to volunteer every Wednesday night, and now their family members have started to join them.

Bard on the Beach is not just a highly successful theatre group. In my research for this section on volunteers, I learned that Bard is also a social club (and occasional dating venue) for over 250 people who are engaging with the community, with theatre, and with themselves. In contrast to many other theatre companies, Bard does not employ individuals to work at the concession or as ushers. It does not pay salaries, yet has no problem with the recruitment and retention of a highly talented pool. The fact that so many return year after year, organize their own friendship groups for socializing away from Bard, bake bread and cakes for colleagues and actors, and attest they are impatient for the season to start so they can commit again illustrates the unique organizational culture that Bard, as a not-for-profit business, has achieved and retained over twenty-five years. The volunteers, both past and present, have been instrumental in making Bard affordable and accessible, two of the key objectives Christopher espoused when establishing this company. Their influence and support has been and continues to be of paramount importance.

RIGHT > *Christopher Gaze and Claire Sakaki, 2015.* JASON KEEL

[SCENE IV]

The Quiet Volunteers
(The Board)

"Men of few words are the best men."
HENRY V

While the volunteers described above are the foot soldiers of Bard, there is also a small, dedicated, often overlooked group of generals who give their time in a volunteer capacity to oversee this theatre company: the Board of Directors of Bard on the Beach. The 2016 Board consists of thirteen men and women who are recruited to oversee the administration and financial health of the organization. They meet approximately ten times a year, either at the Bard office or at the Bard Village. Village meet-

ings are scheduled on Tuesdays from 5:30 to 7 PM, to enable members to see the performances they have been instrumental in discussing and supporting prior to production. "Well, why wouldn't you?" asked one Board member.

Board members are recruited in one of three ways: self-submissions, existing Board member recommendations, and through actively seeking individuals with a specific skill set. There are no term limits, but most of the current Board members have served less than four years.

Time commitments for these positions vary. From 2011 to 2013, some members estimated working over thirty hours a week. As the organization has settled, the time commitment has been reduced. There are, of course, benefits associated with this role, as one member described: "The perks of the Bard Board for someone who adores theatre are absolutely, unthinkably superb; to be able to go to a first reading of a play and see the actors grapple with it, and then to go and see it at a dress rehearsal, and then at opening night, and then multiple times through the summer. To see something grow and evolve and develop is a superb experience."

The Board at Bard in its first ten to twenty years of existence was a stable group of individuals who oversaw the administration of a highly successful arts group without major issues. Many of these individuals joined the Board after being invited to do so by Christopher.

There was no mandatory term, and some had been in position for long periods of time. "Many had gone back almost to day one, and there was this institutional knowledge," explained one member. "Christopher brought in different people with different knowledge and it all worked fine."

There have been only five Board Presidents, all of whom have provided support and guidance to the organization as it has grown. Grant Burnyeat (1990–1991) was instrumental in the creation and first years of Bard's growth. Andrew Seal (1992–1993) guided the Company through its early rapid growth and was succeeded in 1994 by Ken Affleck, who remained Bard President until 2008, as the Company grew significantly in size and repertoire. John McCulloch took over in 2008, replaced in 2013 only when he took the unusual step of agreeing to fill the position of interim Managing Director at Bard to address serious organizational and financial challenges (see Act II). At that time, Jim Bovard agreed to become President and remains in the role today.

TOP > *Hilde Seal, Andrew Seal (past Board chair), and Darlene Howard (Board member).*

BOTTOM > *Jim Bovard (Board chair), Claire Sakaki (Executive Director), Tony Knox, and Margie Knox (Board vice-chair).*

As Bard grew, it was determined that different sub-committees were needed to deal with the ever-increasing range of activities such as fundraising (a real priority when Bard recognized the need for a new Mainstage tent and replacement of the Douglas Campbell tent). In 2008, a number of long-standing Board members left and were replaced by individuals who had specific skill sets needed by an enterprise in rapid development.

Similar to the 250 volunteers who provide the front-of-house faces most patrons are acquainted with, the frequently overlooked Board members are also a highly cohesive group (five women and eight men in 2016) who seem to love volunteering their time and expertise. In contrast to the administrative management at Bard, this group is composed mostly of men, which, in that respect, is similar to most other boards. While a number do sit on other boards, they describe the Bard Board as being distinctive. "I've sat on a lot of boards and there is a culture at Bard that is quite different to any culture I have ever seen on other boards," remarked one member. "It is open, inclusive, and respectful. These are the three best words to describe it. I see it around the Board table, as they are open to all ideas. You know your idea may not be the one they decide to run with, but they are open to listening, and it's not the same on all boards."

The commitment and love for Bard has been a constant among its Board members, as one of Bard's management team commented:

The Board of Directors then and now is a really good snapshot of the Company's growth. I see that on both sides, from twenty-eight years ago to five years ago, the Board was a dedicated, passionate group of people who wanted to see this Company established, wanted to see this Company survive, and just put everything into it. When the Board started to change—just becoming more sophisticated in terms of how they are formed and nominated and the whole process—that love and commitment stayed. While certain boxes needed to be ticked—they needed to get an accountant on the Board, they needed to get a lawyer on the Board, whatever. The skill set needed to change. Now the Board is a very curated group of people, but they still have that passion and love of the organization.

TOP LEFT ‹ *Associate Artistic Director Dean Paul Gibson, Alice Clarke, Douglas Clarke (Board member), and Christopher Gaze.*

TOP RIGHT ‹ *Long time bookkeeper Renate Ramirez at the Company barbecue in 2003.*

BOTTOM LEFT ‹ *Bard administrative staff at the offices at the BMO Centre, September 2015.*

BOTTOM RIGHT ‹ *Director of Marketing and Communications Heather Kennedy and Associate Artistic Director Dean Paul Gibson.*

[S C E N E   V]

The Audience

"Are you sure that we are awake?
It seems to me that yet we sleep,
we dream."

A MIDSUMMER NIGHT'S DREAM

Whenever I attend theatre, whether it be the Arts Club on Granville Island, student theatre at Langara's Studio 58, or Bard, I study the audience, and it always tends to be older (forty plus), middle-class people. In the summer of 2015, I attended a production in Vancouver on a Saturday night. Limited-view seats were $39, decent seats were over $80. That Saturday night, over 30 percent of the seats were unoccupied. It is a source of constant aggravation to me that many theatre tickets are priced to discourage people from visiting, especially young people. While some theatres do offer student tickets and youth-oriented discounts, I do not understand why more theatres cannot offer reduced prices for other identified limited-income groups. In order to grow our theatre culture and introduce it to everyone, including those who may be new immigrants to Canada, those with limited financial resources, and those who have never experienced the delights of a live performance, theatre must be accessible and affordable. In 2016, the price of tickets to attend Bard theatre productions started at $20. Youth pricing at $29 for every seat is also available. Bard welcomes its audience by making itself accessible and affordable. This was one of its founding goals and remains so today. As a new immigrant to Canada in 1992, with little spare money, I could not afford to attend many of the productions at other established Vancouver venues, but I could attend Bard. I attended in 1992 for the first time and have attended most of the plays staged since then. And as my affluence level has grown, I am now a donor. I choose to give back to the organization that gave me the opportunity to see theatre when money was not plentiful, and I do not believe I am unique in this.

Many of those who regularly attend Bard performances or who volunteer their time are also donors. Their financial gifts support the not-for-profit theatre company, not only ensuring affordable, high-standard Shakespeare productions can be offered in Vancouver, but also enabling innovative educational programs to exist (see Act V). As a member of management confirmed, "Bard has been very lucky to have a large and loyal membership base who are truly invested in the growth and success of the festival."

Each year, Bard conducts surveys to gather data on its patrons. In 2015, 38 percent

PAGES 155–158 › *Audience members of all ages.*

PAGE 158, BOTTOM › *Alexandra Eaton, Sarah Harrison, John-Paul Radelet, and Alison Knight (Riotous Youth, 2014).*

had attended for over ten years, with 98 percent saying they had attended at least one previous season. Many stated that their attendance was part of a yearly established tradition. In 2015, only 10 percent of those who responded to the survey were first-time attendees. Almost 90 percent felt the price they paid was fair for the experience gained, confirming that Bard was still delivering on its mandate.

Particular thought is given to how to attract the younger professionals and the eighteen- to thirty-year-olds, especially as Bard's stable demographic "ages out." Explained one Board member, "I've seen the age demographic at Bard coming down. Bard's raison d'être is not to raise money; its raison d'être is to teach people about Shakespeare, to educate, and entertain. Bard doesn't look to commercialism, it looks at how it can be accessible to today's crowd. So the fact we do *Taming of the Shrew* as a spaghetti western is not commercial, it's creative, it's making it accessible, it's how do you get the younger generation into theatres."

Others commented on how recent contemporary interpretations of Shakespeare's classics, such as 2015's steampunk *The Comedy of Errors,* and 2016's *The Merry Wives of Windsor,* set in the 1960s, were successful choices for attracting a younger crowd. With youth ticket pricing and a number of $20 seats in every house, Bard is actively trying to bring in the younger generation.

One actor also commented on the audience loyalty that Bard annually attracts, with the challenge being how to reach the population who do not attend. While a few patrons see all of the plays, the majority come only once and feel this annual visit fulfills their summertime "Bard experience." As a member of management confirmed, "About 10 percent of our audience comes and sees everything, then about 80 percent says, 'I want to go to Bard and just see one.' They say, 'Check, I've had my Bard experience for the summer.'" This fact surprised me; I presumed patrons would come more than once, especially since the season is long.

The attraction of new patrons is always a challenge, not only for Bard but for all arts organizations who compete for the population's disposable income. It takes a considerable amount of time and repeat messaging, which Bard has been successfully doing for over a quarter of a century. During the course of writing this book, I spoke to friends, acquaintances, and strangers about my involvement with Bard and was consistently surprised by how many either did not know of it or, if they did, had never attended a performance. My amazement was reflected by others, such as a Board member who said, "I know a lot of people who do not go to Bard, and I say, 'What do you mean, you've never been to Bard? Do you live in this city?'"

Despite the challenges, Bard's performances frequently sell out and achieve overall season capacity of 85 percent or more. Most theatres would be extremely jealous of these numbers.

There is a special, often overlooked, reciprocal relationship between actors and their audience. A couple of performers expressed a preference for appearing on the smaller Howard Family Stage because it of the greater intimacy with the audience. Others remarked on the way Shakespeare's words create more rapport between player and patron than do scripts of other works. "You develop more with an audience with a Shakespeare play than you do with audiences who see other plays," shared one actor. "The characters have a more direct relationship with the audience, you talk directly to them. For example, in *King Lear*, Edmund is the bad guy, but the first thing he does when he's alone is he talks to the audience. Shakespeare contextualizes things in *Othello*. Iago talks directly to the audience. The audience has a greater access to the characters."

Another actor ruminated interestingly on the way the audience influences the delivery of a production. Frequently it is assumed that a play remains constant from opening night in June until closing night in September. But a Board member told me he advises everyone to see a performance at the beginning and end of the season "because just seeing it change is one of the revelations of theatre."

This is recognized by actors as well. "Performances change because the audience tells us a huge amount of what we need to know," explained one actor. "A play

is not complete until there is an audience—it's a crucial ingredient; without them, it's just a rehearsal. So with comedy, until you guys are in front of us, laughing or not, and telling us what's funny or not, we really don't know what we have. If suddenly the audience is laughing when we don't expect it, it makes us stop and think and say, 'Of course, it's funny,' but often we don't see it. And then you start finding other stuff that is funny, and you start looking for other stuff you could have missed. You learn stuff. On closing night, I often realize something and think, 'Oh that's what that is . . . Gosh, I wish I had known that on opening night.' It's always an evolution."

This interaction, albeit subtle, is enhanced at Bard as it is not a traditional enclosed theatre. Performing outside, actors can see the audience when it is light outside, and audience members can easily see their cohort. Traditional theatres are dark and do not offer this. As one actor explained, when it's light outside and "we can see everybody and they can see us; the separation of the veil between the wall is much thinner. Especially in the Douglas Campbell Theatre, where everyone is very close around, there is no barrier—and that makes it special."

Of course, performing in a tent can be challenging for actors and the audience, as both may be distracted by events occurring offstage that are easily audible. Heavy rain crashing on the canvas makes listening very difficult, the party boat playing "YMCA" at full volume as it sails past can-

not be ignored, and police and ambulance sirens puncture the dialogue. "In *Love's Labour's Lost*," recalled one actor, "there was this tough scene when an actor had to cry for her dead father, and outside there was a truck backing up—beep—beep—beep—that is not ideal." A volunteer recalled a time when a woman's cellphone "went off in Juliet's death scene, and she couldn't find it. For weeks afterwards, Christopher told the story and added that if she had been in an aisle seat, there would have been another death." Such interruptions have been present since Bard started way back in 1989. They are just another characteristic that makes it unique.

Bard slowly and cautiously introduced Shakespeare to its audience and made it accessible, not incomprehensible. It employs highly qualified, accomplished actors and technical support staff, in addition to a management team and a huge bank of volunteers, who all work with a sincere love of the organization and a commitment to its goals. By making Shakespeare fun, affordable, understandable, and inspirational, and by delivering high-quality, dynamic productions in an unconventional environment, audiences became loyal and remain so. They are committed to returning. Bard has consistently delivered on the objectives it had from inception: to deliver affordable, accessible Shakespeare in a tent by the ocean. While the numbers tasked with delivering these goals have significantly grown, the commitment to these core values remains. ▶

ACT V

"Why, then the world's mine oyster."

THE MERRY WIVES OF WINDSOR

The PLOT

DEVELOPMENT

[S C E N E 1]

Bard Education

"O this learning, what a thing it is!"

THE TAMING OF THE SHREW

Now for the surprise Act. This section of the book outlines the way this unique theatre company is leaving an indelible mark not only on Vancouver and the Canadian arts scene, but upon the young people who are lucky enough to grow up in this province and have the opportunities to be exposed to Bard on the Beach.

As I mentioned earlier, I have always known about Bard, but in 2009, as a heavily stressed mother of two young boys, anticipating a summer consisting of twelve weeks of unsupervised time, I learned about Bard's summer workshop programs for youth. My firstborn, Jack, was in grade six and had made friends with twins who had attended Bard's two-week Young Shakespeareans Workshop the previous summer and intended to repeat the experience. Jack also expressed an interest, and whether this was due to his interest in theatre (perhaps my prodding had at long last taken effect) or because of the twins, I did not question. I telephoned the twins' mother and quickly learned it was not so easy to gain a place in the much-coveted Young Shakespeareans. The program was so popular that families needed to enter a registration draw several months in advance of the program, and if you weren't lucky, you might get your second or third choice for a workshop. Despite some sleepless nights, I am happy to report all was worthwhile, as Jack did gain a place.

"It's always been a tricky process, ensuring fairness when the demand exceeds our capacity," explained long-time Director of Education, Mary Hartman. "But since one of our Company's core values is accessibility, we've embraced that principle in terms of access to our programs. So no one gets special treatment—my own children went into the lottery along with everyone else, and most years, we ended up with our second choice. Not even our Board members are given priority, and their children and grandchildren are treated like all other participants. It's only fair. We plan to switch to a first-come, first-served approach, but only when we can be sure that access is equal to all."

Bard on the Beach offers a tremendous instructional and fun resource. Again, I wonder whether any other city in Canada (and maybe North America) can boast such a comprehensive range of Shakespearean education, accessible to every student, irrespective of means. In 2016, 4,841 young people attended a Bard education workshop. This wide-ranging education includes:

ONE *Young Shakespeareans Workshops:* Summer camps and year-round workshops for youth aged eight to eighteen.

TWO *Bard in the Classroom:* Workshops in the classroom for elementary and high school children in the BC school system.

THREE *Bard Unbound Workshops:* Professional development for BC teachers.

FOUR *Bard in Your Neighbourhood:* Working with community groups to develop customized programs specifically for their needs, at no cost to the participants or organizations.

FIVE *Riotous Youth:* Education, employment, and mentorship for students aged eighteen to twenty-four.

SIX *Bard for Life:* Recreational workshops in Shakespearean performance for adults.

SEVEN *Bard Studio:* Professional development for theatre artists.

EIGHT *Bard Explored:* Talks on the season's four productions.

NINE *Bursaries* totalling over $21,000 (2016).

YOUNG SHAKESPEAREANS WORKSHOPS

In 1995, Moira Wylie, the wife of Douglas Campbell, who was working at Bard at the time, established an initiative encouraging the introduction of young people to Shakespeare through workshops during the summer months. Over the course of the last twenty years, her legacy and this program have slowly grown, with over three hundred students between the ages of eight and eighteen now taking part each year.

The aim of these workshops is to offer students an introduction to Shakespeare that is engaging, enlightening, and rewarding. Creativity, fun, exploration, and playfulness are encouraged while students are actively involved in studying "the Bard," through drama exercises and learning scripts and acting techniques. Students aged eight to thirteen are enrolled for three hours a day over a two-week period, while those aged thirteen to eighteen are enrolled for four hours a day. All workshops take place during the summer months on the Bard stages. There are sixteen participants in each group, and workshops are led by two teaching artists. These teaching artists are theatre professionals, such as actors or directors, who work with the students on a specific play. Many are actors from the Bard Company, supported by students in the Riotous Youth program who are looking at ways to support their chosen careers in this comprehensive field (see Riotous Youth section below).

In 2016, twenty-seven workshops were offered. The number varies slightly each year and is dependent on stage space, as the workshops take place on the two Festival stages. When this space is not needed by the Bard cast, it can be used for these workshops. It is easy to understand why kids love this environment, where they can run around and have access to the actual Bard stage, in front of all the empty seats that later that day will be occupied by audience members. This is a far cry from the aged, dilapidated school auditorium, smelling of sweaty bodies and overseen by a school teacher whose first love may not be classical theatre. This is an actual, real theatre, with instruction from a theatre professional and contemporaries who are enthusiastic to be there.

"It was the first time I had the opportunity to talk to other people my age who are passionate about Shakespeare," shared one Young Shakespearean workshop participant. "And it was the first time I was in a 'class' situation and the text wasn't presented in an intimidating manner. Also, the way the parts were divided was great." Another recalled, "I liked how well we worked together as a group, despite the age difference (I'm thirteen and was working with eight-year-olds). I like that we got to put in our own ideas for each scene, we got to choose our characters, and how creative the instructors were and how creative they let us be."

A one-week intensive workshop (seven hours each day) is also offered for students aged fifteen to eighteen. At the completion of all workshops, the students perform for their parents and friends. Registration in the program also comes with two tickets to a Mainstage performance.

Another Young Shakespearean Workshop participant beautifully articulated the appeal of Shakespeare for the younger generation:

> *Shakespeare's stories are really exciting, with such variety, that you're always able to find something new and interesting. And the language is incredible. From the ages of eight to eighteen, you're going through a huge range of emotions, and when you find Shakespeare, you see things you can really relate to. Shakespeare isn't elitist or academic; he's just about human emotions, and young people connect with that. We understand what he's saying, but, more importantly, we get how it feels, because we're going through it in real life. And then in Young Shakespeareans, you get to experience all of that in this safe, supporting community of really amazing people.*

TOP ‹ *A Nutshell talk in the Village, 2015.*

BOTTOM ‹ *An all-ages BMO Mainstage talk, Family Night, 2015.*

The workshops have also been expanded to run during Spring Break, and in 2016 Bard began offering classes on Saturdays. Costs are similar to comparable theatre/acting courses in the Lower Mainland. I have the impression that no matter how much this program is expanded, demand will always outstrip supply. Recognizing that the costs of some of these workshops could be prohibitive, Bard created a bursary fund. As Mary Harlman, long-standing Director of Education at Bard explained, it was the volunteers who decided to give their tips to start a bursary program. "Those working in the concession were offered tips, and of course it was unfair for some to get tips and others not, so the tips would all be pooled until the end of the summer and the volunteers would vote for what they wanted to do with it. But in 2009, the volunteers got the idea they wanted to establish a Young Shakespeareans bursary, and that was about $1,000 to $1,200. So a bursary fund was established and it was really great . . . In 2015 the volunteers agreed the tips should go to the bursary fund at the start of the season, so we were able to put up signs. And then all events where we didn't have the concession open, we would have tea and coffee available, with donations going to the bursary fund, including the 10 AM Young Shakespearean presentation, so for those parents to have coffee was a real good thing." In 2016, over $21,300 in bursaries were awarded to students.

BARD IN THE CLASSROOM

Offered since 2006, this initiative sees two teaching artists visit schools throughout the Lower Mainland to lead interactive workshops within a classroom environment, with the objective of introducing students to the language, character, and ideas of the plays. Approximately 180 of these workshops are offered per year to schools, home learners, and community groups, for up to thirty-five participants, grades K to twelve (as well as to adults), and are tailored to fit the needs of the group. Some workshops provide a general introduction to Shakespeare, others focus on a specific play or more in-depth analysis of scenes and characters and are designed with input from the school. Often, the plays chosen reflect the school curriculum or those in the current Bard season. Schools pay for this initiative through school budgets, student activity fees, Parent Advisory Council funding, and sometimes through the students themselves. They may also be funded through the educational bursary, as the Bard website states:

> We understand that it's difficult for schools to find the funds for this sort of experience, so we are eager to work with you to find a way to visit your class. We have established an Education Bursary Fund to help eliminate the financial barriers to participation, and have dedicated a significant portion of this year to help schools.

BARD UNBOUND WORKSHOPS

Related to Bard in the Classroom is a component offering professional development for classroom teachers. Designed primarily for high-school language arts as well as literature and drama teachers, the objective is to provide teachers with the techniques for exploring and understanding Shakespeare—teaching the teachers. Workshops are offered on professional development days and given by Bard's Director of Education. In 2016, forty-seven teachers took part. The workshops were extended from half a day to a full day in 2016 and can be custom-designed to focus on a specific play or to serve a particular school district.

BARD IN YOUR NEIGHBOURHOOD

This relatively new initiative was introduced as a pilot project in 2015 and seeks to work with community partners to bring Bard workshops to underserved youth at no cost, with the objective of engaging children in the creative participation and enjoyment of Shakespeare. The initiative runs in roughly the same way as Bard in the Classroom, with teaching artists visiting alternative schools, often where

TOP ➤ *Jennifer Gaze and granddaughter Stella at Family Night, 2016.*

BOTTOM ➤ *Mainstage Theatre tent audience, 2013.*

there is a high student–teacher ratio and students who may have challenges fitting into the regular school system. Teaching artists offer introductory workshops, and if a positive experience is gained, a longer residency can be created. Bard provides all funds for this initiative.

RIOTOUS YOUTH

This program grew out of the Young Shakespeareans program in 2014. At that time, some of the Young Shakespeareans who had been involved with the program for over ten years articulated to Bard administration a desire to continue their involvement with Bard after the age of eighteen. From this, Riotous Youth was born. "It emerged from participants, which is I think one of the strengths of the program," explained a member of management. "There were so many [Young] Shakespeareans who were so committed. They had been doing it for ten years and really loved it, and kind of wanted to stay involved in some way, so we felt we needed to test this out . . . It started with a couple of individuals and then [we] decided that we needed to make it into a program."

The program offers internships and apprenticeships for former Young Shakespeareans and others aged nineteen to twenty-four. Riotous Youth interns attend classes led by teaching artists from Bard and assist with the teaching in the Young Shakespeareans program. Twenty applicants vied for the coveted nine places in the 2015 program. That year, the students asked if they could be allocated a mentor to work with, so this grassroots, student-led suggestion was incorporated, again reflecting the openness of the organization. In addition, the Bard staff were aware that their young prodigies needed funding, so in 2016, participants also worked in the box office, as clerical support, or with the artistic team, thereby gaining a wage and valuable, relevant, practical work experience. The Riotous Youth program offers participants a balance between teaching the younger students involved in other programs, receiving instruction on voice, text, and acting skills through performances, receiving mentorship, and gaining relevant, paid work experience. The Riotous Youth also deliver the "In a Nutshell" pre-performance introductory talks, which take place in the Bard Village, thus honing public speaking skills.

Riotous Youth is a unique early-career development program (no similar programs appear to be offered by other theatre companies) and a direct result of Bard listening and responding to students requesting more.

BARD FOR LIFE

In 2016, the inaugural Bard for Life program was offered. Similar to Young Shakespeareans, but for adults, this program offers fourteen participants the opportunity to work with two Bard teaching artists one evening a week for eight weeks. Participants ranging in age from their late thirties to late eighties take part in acting exercises, playing roles, and trying their hand at performing Shakespeare. This newer initiative again illustrates that Bard's commitment to education is not just geared to the young, but to the entire community.

BARD STUDIO

In addition to the primary outreach programs outlined above, when Bard became established in its new home in 2016, it was able to offer free drop-in programs for theatre professionals within the new rehearsal space and classrooms. This initiative, called Bard Studio, includes classes for voice, movement, acting, and teaching and is open to both emerging and established theatre professionals. Its objective is to "enrich the professional skills and extend the collaboration in the Metro Vancouver theatre community," thereby also enriching the cultural life of the city. "We have a responsibility to give back, by what we are able to do in this building, back to the arts community," explained a member of management. "In the past, we have not had resources we could share to help others because we were in temporary locations. Now we have a rehearsal space and a costume collection, and it's easily accessible. We have resources to help others."

BARD LAB

Another result of Bard being granted a new permanent home was that it was able to establish a new program called the Bard Lab. Over the years, Christopher has been presented with a number of ideas for exploratory works, and while the Board's Artistic Goals Committee recognized this need a number of years ago, for various reasons, the funding was not available.

In 2005, Bard first moved away from the canon and offered non-Shakespearean (but related) works. That programming variation has occurred from time to time in the years since. Then, in early 2016, individuals within the artistic community were invited to present proposals for plays, performances, and Shakespeare-related ideas. After reviewing these proposals, a panel of local artists made recommendations on initiatives it would like to fund, and the idea behind the Bard Lab finally reached fruition. It is hoped that something "homegrown" may be the result of the lab. One respondent suggested a two- to three-person show, which would "slide into the schedule at the end of the season," while another suggested performances during the intermission. "Maybe something evolves and ends up on the Mainstage," offered one Board member. "It's the perfect balance, where you can stretch artistically but be fiscally responsible." There is considerable excitement over this young initiative, which aims to plant seeds and see what grows. It is also a way for the wider artistic community to access Bard's resources. "It's a reason for diversifying. It's a gift, this place, and we have to share it," explained one actor/director. "We must share our good fortune and make sure this is an open-door performance space. We are looking for all kinds of ways for the artists to create and share their works."

BARD EXPLORED

On four Saturday mornings each summer, sixty-minute talks on the plays being performed are given by an expert in the field, frequently an academic from a local college or university. During these presentations, Shakespeare's inspirations and influences are reviewed, with the opportunity for participants to have questions answered and thereby receive a fuller understanding and appreciation of the season's plays.

AUDIENCE EDUCATION

In addition to its formal classroom teachings, Bard educates audiences through its performances, by introducing us to new and innovative interpretations of Shakespeare, stretching traditional boundaries. One actor/director, in describing Bard's evolution away from "a traditional conservative company" in terms of the productions offered, commented, "We started in an 'English' way, and we've happily moved away from those trappings, which were lovely and quaint, but we've evolved artistically . . . While there are those who are tremendously offended that we do alternative productions, there are others who say, "Wow—that's Shakespeare.' It's imperative for artists to have freedom to explore and conceptualize the stories for the contemporary world."

Over the years, the interpretations of the plays selected by the Artistic Director have become more adventurous, taking Bard away from preconceived notions, as in setting *Love's Labour's Lost* in the 1930s, or offering *The Comedy of Errors* with a steampunk theme. Actors also commented on how their education has been enhanced through their involvement with Bard. As one offered, "Once you do them and get into them, you love them for different reasons. You start to appreciate the broad, wild quality of some of the stories, and appreciate the thought and the consideration. It's been a massive education for me."

[S C E N E I I]

The Future

"Why, then the world's mine oyster."

THE MERRY WIVES OF WINDSOR

I wonder how many of Bard's patrons are aware of the wider impact this theatre company is having on the young population of Vancouver, particularly upon those who want to pursue a career in the arts, but even upon those who, like my son, just have an interest in theatre. By going beyond their initial remit and investing in an extensive and expanding educational program, Bard has successfully in introduced distinctive, relevant, and vibrant programs for schools and community groups. While eliminating education programs is often one of the first cost-cutting measures for cash-strapped groups (as when the Vancouver Playhouse was going through financial difficulties), Bard's commitment to education has been constant throughout its almost thirty-year history.

For many high-school students in Vancouver, some of whom may be first-generation immigrants, theatre (and particularly Shakespeare) can be an alien, difficult concept whose origins are in an entirely different four-hundred-year-old culture. All students are required to study Shakespeare's plays in the grade ten BC curriculum onwards (and sometimes before), and yet many fifteen-year-olds see it as an old, worthless, boring, and alienating experience. With these students (and their parents), who may never have been exposed to theatre, in mind, Bard has created outreach programs that actively encourage young people to engage in and attend English theatre through Bard productions to help break down resistance to theatre. Currently, while lucky students in Greater Vancouver have opportunities to experience Bard, those in the rest of the province do not. There is a huge potential for Bard to extend its educational component to other regions through remote learning initiatives.

One Bard volunteer captured the educational value of Bard when she said, "I believe plays have to be seen as well as read. I was an English teacher, and I brought my students [to the plays]. I believed the study of Shakespeare was important and could be a wonderful experience, if handled right. I was right. I brought my students, and even had Christopher come and talk to two of my classes to discuss his version of *Richard III*. It was a wonderful experience for my students."

At this time in Bard's life, it is doubtful that the number of performances will increase. The physical space of the Bard Village and the constant climatic factors mean that the performance schedule cannot be extended. The area of the organization that shows the most potential for growth may be the educational components, as Bard creates and fosters an active group of young people who are just as committed to Shakespeare as the older patrons who attend plays each year. This was recognized by many I interviewed, who, when asked about changes or developments they would like to see, suggested that Bard increase involvement within the community through educational programs, not just for youth but for other groups, such as lawyers (by teaching the art of presenting in court), and business managers (by teaching how to create relationships of trust). Adult/senior education could also be expanded through the Bard Explored program, as this is a growing demographic, with more retirees looking for opportunities to expand their knowledge on Bard, perhaps even via the production and performance of plays themselves. Board members recognizing that Bard should be known for its education of youth and artists seemed keen to explore investment and commitment to the broader arts community.

Very few of the over two hundred students who attend Young Shakespeareans each year will want to go on and pursue a career in the arts (my son is now at university studying sciences), but this early introduction to Shakespeare as a fun, interactive, non-threatening art form, whether through workshops or supporting teachers in the classroom, enables children to receive exposure to theatre and no longer regard it as a foreign, uninteresting concept. A Board member, in articulating other reasons an education at Bard is beneficial, suggested, "It teaches tolerance, it teaches against discrimination, it teaches patience, expands language and public speaking skills, and it encourages confidence and creativity. This is what the arts do. It is the soft skills that are being forgotten behind math and science, but it is the soft skills which are necessary to hold your life together. The fact Bard is investing in education by teaching Shakespeare is huge. It's huge."

In 2016, over $21,000 was awarded in bursaries assisting over 1,100 students. Who knew? It is these students of today who will grow into the patrons of tomorrow, but only if they understand and appreciate the art. By investing in education, Bard is encouraging and engendering a love of theatre and securing its future. This is not only good for the wider arts community but is also a savvy business move. The new offices housing the Arts Club and Bard offer a training and educational facility unique to the arts community in Vancouver that is set to be developed as its tenure increases. As one Board member confirmed, "We are always thinking about expanding, and we are now at a point when we are able to actively think of expanding. That is what is special about this new location."

Hopefully, when the second edition of this book is published, Bard's educational component will be as well known as its theatrical productions. Theatre is one of the oldest art forms and should be encouraged and supported. Bard's commitment to first-rate performances is well known. Its far-reaching, diverse, multi-faceted educational component is not. This is where the plot should develop. This is the future of Bard. ►

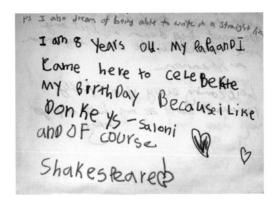

▲ *Note from a young Bard fan at a performance of* A Midsummer Night's Dream.

BARD ON THE BEACH

SHAKESPEARE FESTIVAL

BMO MAINSTAGE

"*The web of our life is of a mingled yarn, good and ill together.*"

ALL'S WELL THAT ENDS WELL

EPILOGUE

As I stated in the Prologue, I was more than a little apprehensive about starting this project, not only because of a perceived ignorance and lack of formal training in the arts, but because, compared with my recent experience as a travel writer, I did not think it would be fun, rewarding, or sexy. Could hanging around with actors, directors, Board members, and management officials, talking about being in a tent, really be as stimulating as taking international flights to foreign countries, staying in designer hotels and writing about Budapest, Rome, or New York, or driving around the province of British Columbia exploring the breathtaking outdoors? But meeting with Christopher Gaze and Claire Sakaki changed my mind. I then spoke to over forty individuals closely associated with Bard on the Beach, and transcribed over one hundred hours of interviews. I was welcomed into this family with open arms. And it *is* a family. That analogy was offered to me on countless occasions, from every level of the organization. As one Board member explained, "Bard's customers are fearlessly committed to Bard. I think it comes back to culture, I really do. I think everyone that goes to Bard feels part of the family, and that's how they are treated by the volunteers at Bard. Christopher Gaze makes the announcement from the stage virtually every night, and everyone is made to feel part of that family." It is this analogy that forms the structure of this Epilogue—the final stage of a play that comments on and summarizes the main action.

After being offered "a seat at the table," listening to animated conversations, the sibling rivalries, the children's teasing, the senior members' ramblings, and stories of engagements, weddings, breakups, divorces, and deaths, I feel privileged to have gained special insight into my adopted kin. As acceptance of my presence grew, I was surprised by how quickly I was able to relay stories to long-term members concerning the entertaining antics of various aunts, uncles, distant cousins, and the black sheep. I could remember forgotten anecdotes and add meat to the bones of half-remembered recollections because I had lived among many generations and been given their confidences, while at the same time offering undivided rapt attention. I did not need to feign interest while looking at the aged family album and numerous baby photographs, nor stifle yawns when shown souvenirs and memorabilia. It was all fascinating to me, and I knew it would be to others. After long marriages, wives tire of their spouse's stories told with stunning regularity during dinner parties and social occasions. I arrived enthusiastic to listen and learn. I found myself in a role similar to a new girlfriend who, upon the all-important first encounter with her lover's parents, pays attention to every detail of the meeting, desperate to be met with approval. It is now time to spill the beans and offer my understanding on what makes Bard on the Beach the very special family unit it is.

There are four traits—distinctively unique characteristics—I can identify from my experience living among the Bard on the Beach family: culture (family bonding and upbringing); finances (the housekeeping budget); accessibility (extended family and friends); and location (the family's homes).

CULTURE
(Family Bonding and Upbringing)

Bard has a unique organizational culture, a topic well covered in the academic business literature analyzing the success of some organizations over the failure of others. I wonder how many more of those associated with Bard I would have needed to talk with before finding someone who offered negative comments about Bard's culture.

(During the course of the interviews, the *only* major issue respondents expressed dissatisfaction with was the weather and the related challenges of delivering a quality service while working in the elements. While this affected their work, all acknowledged that it was not in their control, with many adding that on warm, sunny days, working outside in a tented environment was a wonderful experience.)

One of the key factors that studies on organizational culture acknowledge is the influence leaders (father figures) can have on their environments. While Douglas Campbell's friendship, mentorship, and advice to Christopher to "do something" were profound, it was Christopher's decision alone to follow this guidance. Without Christopher Gaze, Bard on the Beach would not exist.

Everyone likes Christopher Gaze, the father of Bard on the Beach (despite the fact, as mentioned in Act I, he occasionally cheats at golf). Everyone has the utmost respect and appreciation for the man himself, his limitless energy and enthusiasm, his charismatic personality, his commitment to the theatre he created, and his involvement in the wider community. He has achieved a truly remarkable feat by taking a small idea, growing it into a huge success (without significant government assistance) and, in so doing, fostering a working environment adored by everyone associated with it. Volunteers, employees, actors, directors, designers, and Board members all expressed total commitment to Bard and stated that it could not have reached this level of success without Christopher Gaze. He has been instrumental in creating the Bard family, its unique culture, and a fantastic tradition for Vancouverites. As one Board member said, "He is the brand. He is the ambassador. He is the Trevor Linden."

An actor/director also weighed in, describing Christopher's enthusiasm for the work and the Company as "really unmatchable. He's so tireless and committed to keeping this thing going, and he does it in a way that is very different to other artistic producers in Vancouver. He is such an incredible face for the Company;

people associate him with this Company so closely." While all of those interviewed agreed that Bard could not have grown without Christopher, most believed it would carry on should he decide to retire. (At time of writing, he has a five-year contract as Artistic Director at Bard and no intention of retiring.)

It would seem the hard work, challenges, and growing pains that all organizations experience when establishing themselves have been addressed. The new permanent location, the secure management structure, and the twenty-eight year history suggest Bard will remain a permanent fixture in Vancouver. The "family name" will live on. But this does not mean the Board has not considered the theatre company without its father. "We did a SWOT (Strength, Weaknesses, Opportunities, Threats) a few years ago," explained a Board member. "The biggest strength was Christopher Gaze, and the biggest weakness was Christopher Gaze, because—to put it bluntly—you are one heartbeat away from what? And for a while there, it would have been oblivion for the organization because it was him. But fortunately, with the growth we have had and with his humility and personality, we are strong."

And Christopher also acknowledges, with characteristic modesty, that despite his being the catalyst, Bard is an entity in its own right. He uses the analogy of the English pub, with patrons who go because they like the proprietor, but which would survive if that individual left.

FINANCES
(The Housekeeping Budget)

The Bard culture, if not unique, is definitely unusual in having such an identifiable leader. But it is also distinct in other ways. Most theatre and arts organizations are not as heavily funded by ticket sales and corporate and individual donations. In 2016, 77 percent of Bard's income was earned revenue (ticket sales, gift shop, concession), 16 percent was gained through fundraising, and only 4 percent from government grants. As one Board member noted, "It is the patrons who have financially helped Bard, not the government, and this is very, very rare." Another Board member echoed this, saying, "I know so many not-for-profits and their first step is, 'Hello government, can you give us some money?' Bard hasn't relied on this funding." The list of corporate and individual donors is long. From the beginning, Christopher has been successful in attracting funds, and continues to be. Although he may prefer to be onstage performing, or offstage directing, he recognizes his talent for attracting money to support the artists and productions he adores is needed even more. In addition to large corporate donors, such as Goldcorp and BMO Financial Group, there are many individuals who give significant sums. There are even more Vancouverites, including a large number of volunteers, who support Bard through purchasing memberships.

One of the real anomalies of Bard has been the lack of Canada Council for the Arts grants. This is a "tricky" issue to write about, as from 2014 through 2017 Bard did receive a small grant ($25,000 each year), so maybe things are changing. But these figures are not significant in comparison to the sums received by other arts organizations, or in comparison to the private and corporate donations Bard receives. Why, when so many theatres across the country receive such a large amount of their operating budget from Canada Council, does Bard get so little?

In 2014, only 1.3 percent of Bard's revenue was achieved from public-sector grants; in 2015, this figure increased slightly, to 3.4 percent. If there is one fact that surprised and annoyed me during the research for this book, it is this lack of government support. I love Bard. I discovered that those working and volunteering at Bard love it too. Over a hundred thousand audience members annually demonstrate their love and affection for Bard by attending shows.

The challenge for Bard is with its current funding structure. This structure is not guaranteed, nor does it constitute a reliable, stable income. It fluctuates based on any number of uncontrollable elements, such as the weather (cold and wet conditions do not sell tickets); bad reviews that may discourage attendance; competition with other arts events in the city; or dramatic events causing cancelled performances (as in 2010 when the tent structure failed). There are many external factors that affect income. Consequently, it is very difficult to operate a $6-million business when over 75 percent of revenue is volatile. This is where government grants come in. Grants sustain an organization. Grants also enable risks to be taken and can be used to develop programs and foster innovative initiatives. Of course, grants can be a double-edged sword. An arts organization does not want to become overly dependent upon them, but at the same time they can provide an all-important cushion against unforeseen circumstances.

ACCESSIBILITY
(Family Bonding and Relationships)

In the Prologue, I admitted I was anything but a Shakespeare buff, but over the course of years in Vancouver, I grew to love Bard from a distance. In all the performances I attended, I was never made to feel ignorant; I always felt included. While I may not have always fully appreciated the individual nuances or full meaning of the more taxing Shakespeare works such as *Pericles*, *Richard III*, or *Titus Andronicus*, I always enjoyed the performances. And so many others I spoke with shared this feeling.

Many actors I interviewed, whether they had appeared on a Bard stage or not, also appreciate Bard on the Beach. Bard has given many artists one of the very few opportunities to perform, in Western Canada, the classical works of the world's greatest playwright.

This Company has made Shakespeare accessible and affordable for everyone: Shakespeare for the masses, as William commanded it to be. Accessibility and affordability were two of Bard's core values from its inception and remain so today. In 2016, a performance could be seen for $20—only slightly higher than the price of a movie ticket (which was the original remit in 1989), and Bard popcorn is far superior (and cheaper) than popcorn purchased in a commercial movie theatre.

Accessibility has been encouraged over the years, as the family has sought to increase its size by demonstrating to others the benefits of inclusion through educational initiatives. This is the future of Bard, as it is in all families, but it is not just young people who have and will continue to receive an education through Bard. As illustrated in Act V, through new initiatives such as the Bard Lab and other outreach programs, the Company is extending open arms and inviting more people into its home.

LOCATION
(The Family's Homes)

Arts groups and their extended families are the lifeblood of a community. When I think about what constitutes a city, it is not just physical buildings and supporting infrastructure. It is walking, going to work, taking the kids to school, riding a bike, eating and drinking in bars and restaurants, taking part in or watching sports, and having access to cultural institutions. Arts communities contribute to a vibrant, livable city, and Bard's new offices offer a fresh space from which to contribute. In its permanent second home—the BMO Theatre Centre—Bard is deeply embedded in the community. People can walk by the large windows and see a costume shop, entrance to the foyer, spacious bar, and kitchen area with actors socializing, and attend matinee and evening performances at the Goldcorp Stage. The family home is right in the midst of apartments, coffee bars, cycling tracks, and dog walkers. Bard is now more than just its temporary summertime presence defined by iconic white tents by the ocean at Vanier Park. After twenty-eight years, an off-season "home sweet home" has at last been achieved.

When I asked interviewees if there was anything they disliked about Bard, almost all mentioned being in the Village when it was cold, wet, and muddy. When I asked them what they liked best and found unique, they often had exactly the same response: Bard's tent location in Vanier Park. This transient tent home is the very essence of this theatre company. Bard is not just about the performance of a Shakespeare play. Bard is an "experience." This experience begins through the Village's iconic wrought iron entranceway (which has been featured on promotional material since the Company started), and continues, after having tickets collected from the quaint box office and being greeted by those happy volunteers, to the white picnic tables or locations on the grass to unpack a picnic among planters of colourful flowers in the delightful Village environment.

Bard is also a wonderful people-watching place: How will that young, skinny woman in the pretty thin-strapped dress survive when the sun goes down? Look at that guy in a tuxedo, and his friend wearing that Hawaiian shirt—such a contrast in attire! There's Christopher Gaze—isn't he wearing well! Pre-performance presentations are enjoyed, refreshments purchased, the cleanest porta-potties on the West Coast can be used and, if you are a long-time resident of Vancouver, friends and acquaintances are encountered: "Didn't know you were a Bard fan!" "Been coming for years; would never miss it."

When the traditional bell is rung by the Village Manager, announcing the imminent start to the performance, red-vested volunteers are on hand to guide you to your seat. You attempt to balance all the belongings brought from your vehicle, in addition to drinks, Bard chocolate (milk, dark, and plain options), and Bard popcorn, while trying to keep up with the spouse. At this point, you may discover that a stranger is occupying your assigned seat and needs to be moved to the adjacent one: "Sorry, didn't have my glasses on. Would you like me to help you with that chocolate/beer/popcorn?" Conversations are begun over which performances have been seen to date, and new friends quickly made.

The audience starts to applaud, the house lights dim (barely noticeable if it's bright outside) and there is a tingling in your senses. Then, as he has done for twenty-eight years, Christopher Gaze (or an actor or a colleague) bounds enthusiastically onto the stage while smiling and mouthing "hellos" to the patrons he recognizes in the audience. Commenting on the weather, promoting the other plays, asking us to invite our friends to come, thanking the season's sponsors, and reminding us to turn off cellphones, Christopher Gaze is beautifully consistent and charismatic in his genuine, heartfelt welcome to us all— no one is excluded. Even his opening remarks are an enjoyable experience as patrons whisper to each other about how Christopher has or hasn't aged over the last year, noticing he now needs glasses but is still able to run up those stairs and speak in that sexy "milk chocolatey" smooth voice. Then, with radiant smile and the unspoken realization we are here because of him and the wonderful idea he had twenty-eight years ago, he politely instructs us to sit back and enjoy tonight's performance.

This is what I think is unique about Bard on the Beach. This is what draws me year after year. After living, breathing, researching, and writing about Bard, I discover I am not alone. Others share this love of our adopted family's home. While we may only occupy the spare room in the basement a few nights a year, when we do, our much-anticipated visit is very, very special. The space is spotless, food has been prepared, and the Bard family greets us with open arms, as if we have never been away. We are home. ►

APPENDICES

Shakespeare Festivals Across the World

As would be expected, the most famous Shakespeare companies and theatres are in England. The Royal Shakespeare Company started in Stratford-upon-Avon in 1879 and is undoubtedly the most famous. Stratford is home to three theatres: the Royal Shakespeare Theatre, the Swan Theatre, and The Other Place (an experimental stage; rsc.org.uk.) England is also home to the Globe Theatre, which opened in 1997 in London on the site of the former Globe Theatre, where Shakespeare originally performed his works (shakespearesglobe.com).

Shakespeare has been performed outdoors in Central Park, New York, since 1956. In 1962, the Delacorte Theater was built, providing a permanent home for the renamed New York Shakespeare Festival (publictheater.org). However, perhaps the most famous venue to see Shakespeare in the United States is at Ashland, Oregon. The Oregon Shakespeare Festival started in 1935 and, other than a brief period during the Second World War, has been running ever since. With three theatres on-site, the season runs from February to October, with most shows in the summer being sold out. In 2016, eleven different productions were staged, but not all were Shakespeare (osfashland.org).

While Shakespeare festivals are held across the world, with his plays performed regularly in English and translated into other languages, Japan has a particular attraction for the Bard. Not far from Tokyo, in Maruyama (over 15,000 kilometres from his birthplace), is the Shakespeare Country Park, a theme park built in 1997 at a cost of $12 million. Featuring a reconstruction of the house where he was born, the park offers Shakespeare's plays that have been translated into Japanese.

Shakespeare Festivals in Canada

It is likely no surprise that the most popular non-Canadian playwright to have works performed in Canada is Shakespeare. According to the website Canadian Theatre Encyclopedia, soldiers from Europe performed snippets of his works as far back as 1780. The first professional theatre company to settle in Canada was Allen's Company of Comedians, who presented Shakespeare as early as 1786. Since that time, Shakespeare has flourished in both English- and French-speaking Canada. In twenty-first-century Canada, there are a number of notable Shakespeare companies operating in Vancouver, Stratford, Saskatchewan, Halifax, Calgary, and Toronto, as well as many smaller ones, in places like Victoria.

Stratford While Bard on the Beach is the most successful Shakespeare company in Western Canada, most Canadians (or at least those who know theatre) would likely identify the Stratford Festival in Stratford, Ontario, as the most famous. Christopher Gaze has described Bard as a "seed of Stratford" and "part of their blood." Stratford's history goes back to 1951, when journalist Tom Patterson recognized the economic hardships his hometown was experiencing. Taking inspiration from the theatre scene in Europe during the Second World War, he decided to act upon his ambition to create an open-air festival of Shakespearean plays. Patterson managed to secure the talents of British director Tyrone Guthrie, who in turn persuaded Sir Alec Guinness to star in Stratford's initial season in 1953. Success was immediate, and the original tent was replaced in 1957 by the Festival Theatre, accommodating 2,262 spectators. Later the Avon Theatre (1,107 capacity) and the Tom Patterson Theatre (494 capacity) were added. In 2002, in celebration of Stratford's fiftieth anniversary, the smaller Studio Theatre was added. Stratford's season runs from April to October and is now one of the biggest Shakespeare festivals in North America (stratfordfestival.ca).

In analyzing the success of Stratford, Guthrie believed timing to be key: Canadian society was firmly behind the initiative, having developed a growing love for theatre. Patterson, meanwhile, suggested that it wasn't just the community's commitment to the festival that helped it succeed, but, inadvertently, its naiveté about theatre and what it would take to establish a successful company. He said, "Had we known beforehand, we would probably have thrown up our hands in holy horror. As it was, we didn't know . . . so we just went ahead and did it." These sentiments were later echoed by Christopher Gaze, when reflecting on Bard's beginnings. Nowadays, Stratford has expanded to offer a broad range of theatre, although always featuring Shakespeare in the mix.

Saskatchewan In 1985, the Shakespeare on the Saskatchewan Festival was established, with a mandate to make Shakespeare enriching and accessible to all. Each summer, two plays are produced and performed in repertory on the banks of the Saskatchewan River, running from early July until mid-August. Like Bard, there is a mainstage tent (known as the Billy Tent in honour of William) with a 282-seat capacity, accompanied by a number of smaller tents known as the Elizabethan Village. The company traces its roots to its founder Gordon McCall (who was also Artistic Director from 1985 to 1991). McCall encouraged a group of actors to put together a production of *A Midsummer Night's Dream* in the summer of 1985. This led to a further seven plays under his stewardship and a national tour of a bilingual production of *Romeo and Juliet* directed by Robert Lepage. Since then, the company has grown and is now a fixture of the Saskatchewan summer (shakespearesask.com).

Halifax Shakespeare by the Sea (SBTS) is an artistic-driven, not-for-profit collaborative organization founded and incorporated in 1994. In that year, a performance of *Twelfth Night* attracted an audience of over three thousand in four days. With such an enthusiastic response, SBTS was created. During its history, over seventy productions have been staged, attended by over 200,000, making it the largest outdoor summer festival east of Montreal. Performances take place from July 1 to Labour Day at Point Pleasant Park, one of Halifax's municipal parks, alongside the Atlantic Ocean with backdrops of forests, forts, and batteries, or within a covered eighty-two-seat showcase theatre, should rain cancel the outdoor performance (shakespearebythesea.ca).

Calgary Theatre Calgary's annual production of one Shakespearean play takes place from mid-June until mid August in Prince's Island Park by the Bow River. The program employs Alberta actors who are graduates of post-secondary theatre training programs, with the aim to mentor, celebrate, and encourage the next generation of theatre artists. Many then move on to perform in mainstage productions (theatrecalgary.com).

Toronto Canada's largest city is home to the Shakespeare in High Park event each summer. Promoting itself as Canada's largest and longest-running professional outdoor theatre experience, the festival is produced by the Canadian Stage Company, which turns thirty-five in 2017, and features a unique amphitheatre with stone steps leading to a wooden stage. Two plays are performed in repertory, with children under fourteen admitted for free and everyone else by donation. Reserved and premium seating is available online for $25. The festival runs for July and August (canadianstage.com).

Victoria The Greater Victoria Shakespeare Festival runs for a three-week period each July, with two productions performed on the grounds of Camosun College in Victoria. Performances take place in the afternoons and evenings (vicshakespeare.com).

Core Interview Questions

The following twelve core questions were asked of all respondents. In some cases, depending on the interviewee's area of expertise and role, additional questions were asked. As is often the case with in-person interviews, additional questions arose as a result of the answers given by respondents.

ONE What is your relationship with Bard?

TWO How many seasons have you been involved?

THREE What is your previous work/ theatre experience?

FOUR What do you do?

FIVE Favourite season—why?

SIX Least favourite—why?

SEVEN Best thing about Bard—why?

EIGHT Worst thing about Bard—why?

NINE How has it changed?

TEN What, if anything, makes it unique/ special?

ELEVEN What, if any, changes would you like to see made?

TWELVE Is there anything you would like to add, or think should be in the book?

Bard on the Beach Theatre Society
Organizational Chart, 2016

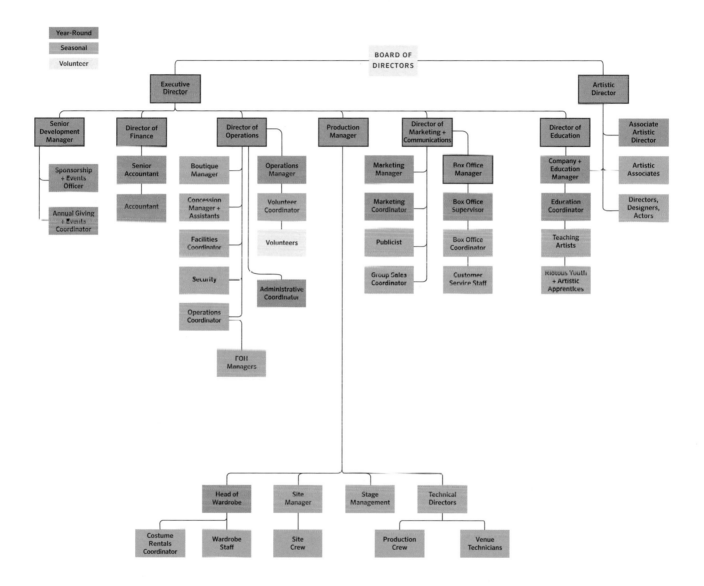

Bard on the Beach
Chronology of Performances

1990 *A Midsummer Night's Dream*

1991 *A Midsummer Night's Dream*
As You Like It

1992 *Twelfth Night*
The Tempest

1993 *The Taming of the Shrew*
Romeo and Juliet

1994 *The Merry Wives of Windsor*
King Lear

1995 *The Comedy of Errors*
Hamlet

1996 *Much Ado About Nothing*
The Merchant of Venice
Shylock (by Mark Leiren-Young)

1997 *Love's Labour's Lost*
The Winter's Tale

1998 *As You Like It*
Richard III

1999 *A Midsummer Night's Dream*
Macbeth
Measure For Measure

2000 *The Tempest*
Henry IV, Part I
All's Well That Ends Well

2001 *The Taming of the Shrew*
Antony and Cleopatra
The Two Gentlemen of Verona

2002 *Twelfth Night*
Henry V
Cymbeline

2003 *The Comedy of Errors*
The Merchant of Venice
Pericles, Prince of Tyre
Shylock (by Mark Leiren-Young)
A Midsummer Night's Dream (Tour)

2004 *Much Ado About Nothing*
The Merry Wives of Windsor
Macbeth

2005 *As You Like It*
Love's Labour's Lost
Hamlet
*Rosencrantz and Guildenstern Are
Dead* (by Tom Stoppard)

2006 *A Midsummer Night's Dream*
Measure For Measure
The Winter's Tale
Troilus and Cressida

2007   *The Taming of the Shrew*
Romeo and Juliet
Julius Caesar
Timon of Athens

2008   *Twelfth Night*
King Lear
The Tempest
Titus Andronicus

2009   *The Comedy of Errors*
Othello
All's Well That Ends Well
Richard II

2010   *Much Ado About Nothing*
Antony and Cleopatra
Falstaff (Henry IV: Parts I & II)
Henry V

2011   *As You Like It*
The Merchant of Venice
Henry VI: The Wars of the Roses
Richard III

2012   *The Taming of the Shrew*
Macbeth
The Merry Wives of Windsor
King John

2013   *Twelfth Night*
Hamlet
Measure For Measure
Elizabeth Rex (by Timothy Findley)

2014   *A Midsummer Night's Dream*
The Tempest
Cymbeline
Equivocation (by Bill Cain)

2015   *The Comedy of Errors*
King Lear
Love's Labour's Lost
Shakespeare's Rebel
     (by C.C. Humphreys)

2016   *The Merry Wives of Windsor*
Romeo and Juliet
Othello
Pericles

2017   *Much Ado About Nothing*
The Winter's Tale
The Merchant of Venice
The Two Gentlemen of Verona
Shylock (by Mark Leiren-Young)

Artistic and Production Timeline *for the 2017 season*

EARLY 2016	Artistic Director selects the five plays and Directors for 2017 season Rights to music and plays (if applicable) secured
MAY 2016	2017 Directors choose set, costume, light, sound designers, fight directors, choreographers Stage Management team selected
JUNE/JULY 2016	General auditions
JULY/AUGUST 2016	Casting auditions
SEPTEMBER/OCTOBER 2016	Actor contracts offered
JANUARY 2017	Preliminary set and costume designs approved
FEBRUARY 2017	Final set and costume designs approved
MARCH 2017	Bard site construction begins in Vanier Park
APRIL 2017	Wardrobe Team begins costume build Set build begins Props build begins Actor intensive BMO Mainstage shows begin rehearsal at BMO Theatre Centre
MAY 2016	Howard Family Stage shows begin rehearsal at BMO Theatre Centre
MAY/JUNE 2017	Set/lighting design install in BMO Mainstage tent
JUNE 2017	Dress rehearsals BMO Mainstage Howard Family Stage tent set/lighting design install
JUNE/JULY 2017	BMO Mainstage shows open
JUNE 2017	Howard Family Stage dress rehearsals
JULY 2017	Howard Family Stage shows open
SEPTEMBER/OCTOBER 2017	Season closes Bard site dismantled and removed from Vanier Park

Founding Members of Bard on the Beach

Christopher Gaze, *Artistic Director*

Kathryn Bracht

Alan Brodie

Marek Czuma

Martin Evans

Bruce Harwood

Corrine Hebden

Laura White

Johnna Wright

Katey Wright

ELIZABETH HADLEY

ABOUT THE AUTHOR

DR. JAYNE SEAGRAVE is a bestselling writer of guidebooks on women's travel and camping, a successful international entrepreneur, and an extensively published academic. She is the author of *Camping British Columbia, the Rockies and Yukon* (now in its eighth edition), *Camping with Kids in the West*, and *Time to Take Flight*. Her infectious energy, joie de vivre, and desire to convey her knowledge, interests, and experience to others have resulted in an eclectic career. Born in England, Jayne moved to Vancouver in 1991 and lives there with her inventor husband, Andrew (with whom she established the Vancouver Tool Corporation), and two teenage sons, Jack and Sam. She spends her spare time in exercise classes, travelling, and enjoying the arts. Learn more at jayneseagrave.com.